CW01024030

Signs of Change

William Morris

CONTENTS

HOW WE LIVE AND HOW WE MIGHT LIVE.

The word Revolution, which we Socialists are so often forced to use, has a terrible sound in most people's ears, even when we have explained to them that it does not necessarily mean a change accompanied by riot and all kinds of violence, and cannot mean a change made mechanically and in the teeth of opinion by a group of men who have somehow managed to seize on the executive power for the moment. Even when we explain that we use the word revolution in its etymological sense, and mean by it a change in the basis of society, people are scared at the idea of such a vast change, and beg that you will speak of reform and not revolution. As, however, we Socialists do not at all mean by our word revolution what these worthy people mean by their word reform, I can't help thinking that it would be a mistake to use it, whatever projects we might conceal beneath its harmless envelope. So we will stick to our word, which means a change of the basis of society; it may frighten people, but it will at least warn them that there is something to be frightened about, which will be no less dangerous for being ignored; and also it may encourage some people, and will mean to them at least not a fear, but a hope.

Fear and Hope—those are the names of the two great passions which rule the race of man, and with which revolutionists have to deal; to give hope to the many oppressed and fear to the few oppressors, that is our business; if we do the first and give hope to the many, the few must be frightened by their hope; otherwise we do not want to frighten them; it is not revenge we want for poor people, but happiness; indeed, what revenge can be taken for all the thousands of years of the sufferings of the poor?

However, many of the oppressors of the poor, most of them, we will say, are not conscious of their being oppressors (we shall see why presently); they live in an orderly, quiet way themselves, as far as possible removed from the feelings of a Roman slave-owner or a Legree; they know that the poor exist, but their sufferings do not present themselves to them in a trenchant and dramatic way; they themselves have troubles to bear, and they think doubtless that to bear trouble is the lot of humanity, nor have they any means of comparing the troubles of their lives with those of people lower in the social scale; and if ever the thought of those heavier troubles obtrudes itself upon them, they console themselves with the maxim that people do get used to the troubles they have to bear, whatever they may be.

Indeed, as far as regards individuals at least, that is but too true, so that we have as supporters of the present state of things, however bad it may be, first those comfortable unconscious oppressors who think that they have everything to fear from any change which would involve more than the softest and most gradual of reforms, and secondly those poor people who, living hard and anxiously as they do, can hardly conceive of any change for the better happening to them, and dare not risk one tittle of their poor possessions in taking any action towards a possible bettering of their condition; so that while we can do little with the rich save inspire them with fear, it is hard indeed to give the poor any hope. It is, then, no less than reasonable that those whom we try to involve in the great struggle for a better form of life than that which we now lead should call on us to give them at least some idea of what that life may be like.

A reasonable request, but hard to satisfy, since we are living under a system that makes conscious effort towards reconstruction almost impossible: it is not unreasonable on our part to answer, "There are certain definite obstacles to the real progress of man; we can tell you what these are; take them away, and then you shall see."

However, I purpose now to offer myself as a victim for the satisfaction of those who consider that as things now go we have at least got something, and are terrified at the idea of losing their hold of that, lest they should find they are worse off than before, and have nothing. Yet in the course of my endeavour to show how we might live, I must more or less deal in negatives. I mean to say I must point out where in my opinion we fall short in our present attempts at decent life. I must ask the rich and well-to-do what sort of a position it is which they are so anxious to preserve at any cost? and if, after all, it will be such a terrible loss to them to give it up? and I must point out to the poor that they, with capacities for living a dignified and generous life, are in a position which they cannot endure without continued degradation.

How do we live, then, under our present system? Let us look at it a little.

And first, please to understand that our present system of Society is based on a state of perpetual war. Do any of you think that this is as it should be? I know that you have often been told that the competition, which is at present the rule of all production, is a good thing, and stimulates the progress of the race; but the people who tell you this should call competition by its shorter name of war if they wish to be honest, and you would then be free to consider whether or no war stimulates progress, otherwise than as a mad bull chasing you over your own garden may do. War or competition, whichever you please to call it, means at the best pursuing your own advantage at the cost of some one else's loss, and in the process of it you must not be sparing of destruction even of your own possessions, or you will certainly come by the worse in the struggle. You understand that perfectly as to the kind of war in which people go out to kill and be killed; that sort of war in which ships are commissioned, for instance, "to sink, burn, and destroy;" but it appears that you are not so conscious of this waste of goods when you are only carrying on that other war called commerce; observe, however, that the waste is there all the same.

Now let us look at this kind of war a little closer, run through some of the forms of it, that we may see how the "burn, sink, and destroy" is carried on in it.

First, you have that form of it called national rivalry, which in good truth is nowadays the cause of all gunpowder and bayonet wars which civilized nations wage. For years past we English have been rather shy of them, except on those happy occasions when we could carry them on at no sort of risk to ourselves, when the killing was all on one side, or at all events when we hoped it would be. We have been shy of gunpowder war with a respectable enemy for a long while, and I will tell you why: It is because we have had the lion's-share of the world-market; we didn't want to fight for it as a nation, for we had got it; but now this is changing in a most significant, and, to a Socialist, a most cheering way; we are losing or have lost that lion's share; it is now a desperate "competition" between the great nations of civilization for the world-market, and to-morrow it may be a desperate war for that end. As a result, the furthering of war (if it be not on too large a scale) is no longer confined to the honour-and-glory kind of old Tories, who if they meant anything at all by it meant that a Tory war would be a good occasion for damping down democracy; we have changed all that, and now it is quite another kind of politician that is wont to urge us on to "patriotism" as 'tis called. The leaders of the Progressive Liberals, as they would call themselves, long-headed persons who know well enough that social movements are going on, who are not blind to the fact that the world will move with their help or without it; these have been the Jingoes of these later days. I don't mean to say they know what they are doing: politicians, as you well know, take good care to shut their eyes to everything that may happen six months ahead; but what is being done is this: that the present system, which always must include national rivalry, is pushing us into a desperate scramble for the markets on more or less equal terms with other nations, because, once more, we have lost that command of them which we once had. Desperate is not too strong a word. We shall let this impulse to snatch markets carry us whither it will, whither it must. To-day it is successful burglary and disgrace, to-morrow it may be mere defeat and disgrace.

Now this is not a digression, although in saying this I am nearer to what is generally called politics than I shall be again. I only want to show you what commercial war comes to when it has to do with foreign nations, and that even the dullest can see how mere waste must go with it. That is how we live now with foreign nations, prepared to ruin them without war if possible, with it if necessary, let alone meantime the disgraceful exploiting of savage tribes and barbarous peoples, on whom we force at once our shoddy wares and our hypocrisy at the cannon's mouth.

Well, surely Socialism can offer you something in the place of all that. It can; it can offer you peace and friendship instead of war. We might live utterly without national rivalries, acknowledging that while it is best for those who feel that they naturally form a community under one name to govern themselves, yet that no community in civilization should feel that it had interests opposed any other, their economical condition being at any rate similar; so that any citizen of one community could fall to work and live without disturbance of his life when he was in a foreign country, and would fit into his place quite naturally; so that all civilized nations would form one great community, agreeing together as to the kind and amount of production and distribution needed; working at such and such production where it could be best produced; avoiding waste by all means. Please to think of the amount of waste which they would avoid, how much such a revolution would add to the wealth of the world! What creature on earth would be harmed by such a revolution? Nay, would not everybody be the better for it? And what hinders it? I will tell you presently.

Meantime let us pass from this "competition" between nations to that between "the organizers of labour," great firms, joint-stock companies; capitalists in short, and see how competition "stimulates production" among them: indeed it does do that; but what kind of production? Well, production of something to sell at a profit, or say production of profits: and note how war commercial stimulates that: a certain market is demanding goods; there are, say, a hundred manufacturers who make that kind of goods, and every one of them would if he could keep that market to himself; and struggles desperately to get as much of it as he can, with the obvious result that presently the thing is overdone, and the market is glutted, and all that fury of manufacture has to sink into cold ashes. Doesn't that seem something like war to you? Can't you see the waste of it—waste of labour, skill, cunning, waste of life in short? Well, you may say, but it cheapens the goods. In a sense it does; and yet only apparently, as wages have a tendency to sink for the ordinary worker in proportion as prices sink; and at what a cost do we gain this appearance of cheapness! Plainly speaking, at the cost of cheating the consumer and starving the real producer for the benefit of the gambler, who uses both consumer and producer as his milch cows. I needn't go at length into the subject of adulteration, for every one knows what kind of a part it plays in this sort of commerce; but remember that it is an absolutely necessary incident to the production of profit out of wares, which is the business of the so-called manufacturer; and this you must understand, that, taking him in the lump, the consumer is perfectly helpless against the gambler; the goods are forced on him by their cheapness, and with them a certain kind of life which that energetic, that aggressive cheapness determines for him: for so far-reaching is this curse of commercial war that no country is safe from its ravages; the traditions of a thousand years fall before it in a month; it overruns a weak or semi-barbarous country, and whatever romance or pleasure or art existed there, is trodden down into a mire of sordidness and ugliness; the Indian or Javanese craftsman may no longer ply his craft leisurely, working a few hours a day, in producing a maze of strange beauty on a piece of cloth: a steam-engine is set a-going at Manchester, and that victory over nature and a thousand stubborn difficulties is used for the base work of producing a sort of plaster of china-clay and shoddy, and the Asiatic worker, if he is not starved to death outright, as plentifully happens, is driven himself into a factory to lower the wages of his Manchester brother worker, and nothing of character is left him except, most like, an accumulation of fear and hatred of that to him most unaccountable evil, his English master. The South Sea Islander must leave his canoe-carving, his sweet rest, and his graceful dances, and become the slave of a slave: trousers, shoddy, rum, missionary, and fatal disease—he must swallow all this civilization in the lump, and neither himself nor we can help him now till social order displaces the hideous tyranny of gambling that has ruined him.

Let those be types of the consumer: but now for the producer; I mean the real producer, the worker; how does this scramble for the plunder of the market affect him? The manufacturer, in the eagerness of his war, has had to collect into one neighbourhood a vast army of workers, he has drilled them till they are as fit as may be for his special branch of production, that is, for making a profit out of it, and with the result of their being fit for nothing else: well, when the glut comes in that market he is supplying, what happens to this army, every private in which has been depending on the steady demand in that market, and acting, as he could not choose but act, as if it were to go on for ever? You know well what happens to these men: the factory door is shut on them; on a very large part of them often, and at the best on the reserve army of labour, so busily employed in the time of inflation. What becomes of them? Nay, we know that well enough just now. But what we don't know, or don't choose to know, is, that this reserve army of labour is an absolute necessity for commercial war; if our manufacturers had not got these poor devils whom they could draft on to their machines when the demand swelled, other manufacturers in France, or Germany, or America, would step in and take the market from them.

So you see, as we live now, it is necessary that a vast part of the industrial population should be exposed to the danger of periodical semi-starvation, and that, not for the advantage of the people in another part of the world, but for their degradation and enslavement.

Just let your minds run for a moment on the kind of waste which this means, this opening up of new markets among savage and barbarous countries which is the extreme type of the force of the profit-market on the world, and you will surely see what a hideous nightmare that profit-market is: it keeps us sweating and terrified for our livelihood, unable to read a book, or look at a picture, or have pleasant fields to walk in, or to lie in the sun, or to share in the knowledge of our time, to have in short either animal or intellectual pleasure, and for what? that we may go on living the same slavish life till we die, in order to provide for a rich man what is called a life of ease and luxury; that is to say, a life so empty, unwholesome, and degraded, that perhaps, on the whole, he is worse off than we the workers are: and as to the result of all this suffering, it is luckiest when it is nothing at all, when you can say that the wares have done nobody any good; for oftenest they have done many people harm, and we have toiled and groaned and died in making poison and destruction for our fellow-men.

Well, I say all this is war, and the results of war, the war this time, not of competing nations, but of competing firms or capitalist units: and it is this war of the firms which hinders the peace between nations which you surely have agreed with me in thinking is so necessary; for you must know that war is the very breath of the nostrils of these fighting firms, and they have now, in our times, got into their hands nearly all the political power, and they band together in each country in order to make their respective governments fulfil just two functions: the first is at home to act as a strong police force, to keep the ring in which the strong are beating down the weak; the second is to act as a piratical body-guard abroad, a petard to explode the doors which lead to the markets of the world: markets at any price abroad, uninterfered-with privilege, falsely called laissez-faire, [13] at any price at home, to provide these is the sole business of a government such as our industrial captains have been able to conceive of. I must now try to show you the reason of all this, and what it rests on, by trying to answer the question, Why have the profit-makers got all this power, or at least why are they able to keep it?

That takes us to the third form of war commercial: the last, and, the one which all the rest is founded on. We have spoken first of the war of rival nations; next of that of rival firms: we have now to speak of rival men. As nations under the present system are driven to compete with one another for the markets of the world, and as firms or the captains of industry have to scramble for their share of the profits of the markets, so also have the workers to compete with each other—for livelihood; and it is this constant competition or war amongst them which enables the profit-grinders to make their profits, and by means of the wealth so acquired to take all the executive power of the country into their hands. But here is the difference between the position of the workers and the profit-makers: to the latter, the profit-grinders, war is necessary; you cannot have profit-making without competition, individual, corporate, and national; but you may work for a livelihood without competing; you may combine instead of competing.

I have said war was the life-breath of the profit-makers; in like manner, combination is the life of the workers. The working-classes or proletariat cannot even exist as a class without combination of some sort. The necessity which forced the profit-grinders to collect their men first into workshops working by the division of labour, and next into great factories worked by machinery, and so gradually to draw them into the great towns and centres of civilization, gave birth to a distinct working-class or proletariat: and this it was which gave them their mechanical existence, so to say. But note, that they are indeed combined into social groups for the production of wares, but only as yet mechanically; they do not know what they are working at, nor whom they are working for, because they are combining to produce wares of which the profit of a master forms an essential part, instead of goods for their own use: as long as they do this, and compete with each other for leave to do it, they will be, and will feel themselves to be, simply a part of those competing firms I have been speaking of; they will be in fact just a part of the machinery for the production of profit; and so long as this lasts it will be the aim of the masters or profit-makers to decrease the market value of this human part of the machinery; that is to say, since they already hold in their hands the labour of dead men in the form of capital and machinery, it is their interest, or we will say their necessity, to pay as little as they can help for the labour of living men which they have to buy from day to day: and since the workmen they employ have nothing but their labour-power, they are compelled to underbid one another for employment and wages, and so enable the capitalist to play his game.

I have said that, as things go, the workers are a part of the competing firms, an adjunct of capital. Nevertheless, they are only so by compulsion; and, even without their being conscious of it, they struggle against that compulsion and its immediate results, the lowering of their wages, of their standard of life; and this they do, and must do, both as a class and individually: just as the slave of the great Roman lord, though he distinctly felt himself to be a part of the household, yet collectively was a force in reserve for its destruction, and individually stole from his lord whenever he could safely do so. So, here, you see, is another form of war necessary to the way we live now, the war of class against class, which, when it rises to its height, and it seems to be rising at present, will destroy those other forms of war we have been speaking of; will make the position of the profit-makers, of perpetual commercial war, untenable; will destroy the present system of competitive privilege, or commercial war.

Now observe, I said that to the existence of the workers it was combination, not competition, that was necessary, while to that of the profit-makers combination was impossible, and war necessary. The present position of the workers is that of the machinery of commerce, or in plainer words its slaves; when they change that position and become free, the class of profit-makers must cease to exist; and what will then be the position of the workers? Even as it is they are the one necessary part of society, the life-giving part; the other classes are but hangers-on who live on them. But what should they be, what will they be, when they, once for all, come to know their real power, and cease competing with one another for livelihood? I will tell you: they will be society, they will be the community. And being society—that is, there being no class outside them to contend with—they can then regulate their labour in accordance with their own real needs.

There is much talk about supply and demand, but the supply and demand usually meant is an artificial one; it is under the sway of the gambling market; the demand is forced, as I hinted above, before it is supplied; nor, as each producer is working against all the rest, can the producers hold their hands, till the market is glutted and the workers, thrown out on the streets, hear that there has been over-production, amidst which over-plus of unsaleable goods they go ill-supplied with even necessaries, because the wealth which they themselves have created is "ill-distributed," as we call it—that is, unjustly taken away from them.

When the workers are society they will regulate their labour, so that the supply and demand shall be genuine, not gambling; the two will then be commensurate, for it is the same society which demands that also supplies; there will be no more artificial famines then, no more poverty amidst over-production, amidst too great a stock of the very things which should supply poverty and turn it into well-being. In short, there will be no waste and therefore no tyranny.

Well, now, what Socialism offers you in place of these artificial famines, with their so-called over-production, is, once more, regulation of the markets; supply and demand commensurate; no gambling, and consequently (once more) no waste; not overwork and weariness for the worker one month, and the next no work and terror of starvation, but steady work and plenty of leisure every month; not cheap market wares, that is to say, adulterated wares, with scarcely any good in them, mere scaffold-poles for building up profits; no labour would be spent on such things as these, which people would cease to want when they ceased to be slaves. Not these, but such goods as best fulfilled the real uses of the consumers, would labour be set to make; for profit being abolished, people could have what they wanted, instead of what the profit-grinders at home and abroad forced them to take.

For what I want you to understand is this: that in every civilized country at least there is plenty for all—is, or at any rate might be. Even with labour so misdirected as it is at present, an equitable distribution of the wealth we have would make all people comparatively comfortable; but that is nothing to the wealth we might have if labour were not misdirected.

Observe, in the early days of the history of man he was the slave of his most immediate necessities; Nature was mighty and he was feeble, and he had to wage constant war with her for his daily food and such shelter as he could get. His life was bound down and limited by this constant struggle; all his morals, laws, religion, are in fact the outcome and the reflection of this ceaseless toil of earning his livelihood. Time passed, and little by little, step by step, he grew stronger, till now after all these ages he has almost completely conquered Nature, and one would think should now have leisure to turn his thoughts towards higher things than procuring to-morrow's dinner. But, alas! his progress has been broken and halting; and though he has indeed conquered Nature and has her forces under his control to do what he will with, he still has himself to conquer, he still has to think how he will best use those forces which he has mastered. At present he uses them blindly, foolishly, as one driven by mere fate. It would almost seem as if some phantom of the ceaseless pursuit of food which was once the master of the savage was still hunting the civilized man; who toils in a dream, as it were, haunted by mere dim unreal hopes, borne of vague recollections of the days gone by. Out of that dream he must wake, and face things as they really are. The conquest of Nature is complete, may we not say? and now our business is, and has for long been, the organization of man, who wields the forces of Nature. Nor till this is attempted at least shall we ever be free of that terrible phantom of fear of starvation which, with its brother devil, desire of domination, drives us into injustice, cruelty, and dastardliness of all kinds: to cease to fear our fellows and learn to depend on them, to do away with competition and build up co-operation, is our one necessity.

Now, to get closer to details; you probably know that every man in civilization is worth, so to say, more than his skin; working, as he must work, socially, he can produce more than will keep himself alive and in fair condition; and this has been so for many centuries, from the time, in fact, when warring tribes began to make their conquered enemies slaves instead of killing them; and of course his capacity of producing these extras has gone on increasing faster and faster, till to-day one man will weave, for instance, as much cloth in a week as will clothe a whole village for years: and the real question of civilization has always been what are we to do with this extra produce of labour—a question which the phantom, fear of starvation, and its fellow, desire of domination, has driven men to answer pretty badly always, and worst of all perhaps in these present days, when the extra produce has grown with such prodigious speed. The practical answer has always been for man to struggle with his fellow for private possession of undue shares of these extras, and all kinds of devices have been employed by those who found themselves in possession of the power of taking them from others to keep those whom they had robbed in perpetual subjection; and these latter, as I have already hinted, had no chance of resisting this fleecing as long as they were few and scattered, and consequently could have little sense of their common oppression. But now that, owing to the very pursuit of these undue shares of profit, or extra earnings, men have become more dependent on each other for production, and have been driven, as I said before, to combine together for that end more completely, the power of the workers—that is to say, of the robbed or fleeced class—has enormously increased, and it only remains for them to understand that they have this power. When they do that they will be able to give the right answer to the question what is to be done with the extra products of labour over and above what will keep the labourer alive to labour: which answer is, that the worker will have all that he produces, and not be fleeced at all: and remember that he produces collectively, and therefore he will do effectively what work is required of him according to his capacity, and of the produce of that work he will have what he needs; because, you see, he cannot use more than he needs—he can only waste it.

If this arrangement seems to you preposterously ideal, as it well may, looking at our present condition, I must back it up by saying that when men are organized so that their labour is not wasted, they will be relieved from the fear of starvation and the desire of domination, and will have freedom and leisure to look round and see what they really do need.

Now something of that I can conceive for my own self, and I will lay my ideas before you, so that you may compare them with your own, asking you always to remember that the very differences in men's capacities and desires, after the common need of food and shelter is satisfied, will make it easier to deal with their desires in a communal state of things.

What is it that I need, therefore, which my surrounding circumstances can give me—my dealings with my fellow-men—setting aside inevitable accidents which co-operation and forethought cannot control, if there be such?

Well, first of all I claim good health; and I say that a vast proportion of people in civilization scarcely even know what that means. To feel mere life a pleasure; to enjoy the moving one's limbs and exercising one's bodily powers; to play, as it were, with sun and wind and rain; to rejoice in satisfying the due bodily appetites of a human animal without fear of degradation or sense of wrong-doing: yes, and therewithal to be well formed, straight-limbed, strongly knit, expressive of countenance—to be, in a word, beautiful—that also I claim. If we cannot have this claim satisfied, we are but poor creatures after all; and I claim it in the teeth of those terrible doctrines of asceticism, which, born of the despair of the oppressed and degraded, have been for so many ages used as instruments for the continuance of that oppression and degradation.

And I believe that this claim for a healthy body for all of us carries with it all other due claims: for who knows where the seeds of disease which even rich people suffer from were first sown: from the luxury of an ancestor, perhaps; yet often, I suspect, from his poverty. And for the poor: a distinguished physicist has said that the poor suffer always from one disease—hunger; and at least I know this, that if a man is overworked in any degree he cannot enjoy the sort of health I am speaking of; nor can he if he is continually chained to one dull round of mechanical work, with no hope at the other end of it; nor if he lives in continual sordid anxiety for his livelihood, nor if he is ill-housed, nor if he is deprived of all enjoyment of the natural beauty of the world, nor if he has no amusement to quicken the flow of his spirits from time to time: all these things, which touch more or less directly on his bodily condition, are born of the claim I make to live in good health; indeed, I suspect that these good conditions must have been in force for several generations before a population in general will be really healthy, as I have hinted above; but also I doubt not that in the course of time they would, joined to other conditions, of which more hereafter, gradually breed such a population, living in enjoyment of animal life at least, happy therefore, and beautiful according to the beauty of their race. On this point I may note that the very variations in the races of men are caused by the conditions under which they live, and though in these rougher parts of the world we lack some of the advantages of climate and surroundings, yet, if we were working for livelihood and not for profit, we might easily neutralize many of the disadvantages of our climate, at least enough give due scope to the full development of our race.

Now the next thing I claim is education. And you must not say that every English child is educated now; that sort of education will not answer my claim, though I cheerfully admit it is something: something, and yet after all only class education. What I claim is liberal education; opportunity, that is, to have my share of whatever knowledge there is in the world according to my capacity or bent of mind, historical or scientific; and also to have my share of skill of hand which is about in the world, either in the industrial handicrafts or in the fine arts; picture-painting, sculpture, music, acting, or the like: I claim to be taught, if I can be taught, more than one craft to exercise for the benefit of the community. You may think this a large claim, but I am clear it is not too large a claim if the community is to have any gain out of my special capacities, if we are not all to be beaten down to a dull level of mediocrity as we are now, all but the very strongest and toughest of us.

But also I know that this claim for education involves one for public advantages in the shape of public libraries, schools, and the like, such as no private person, not even the richest, could command: but these I claim very confidently, being sure that no reasonable community could bear to be without such helps to a decent life.

Again, the claim for education involves a claim for abundant leisure, which once more I make with confidence; because when once we have shaken off the slavery of profit, labour would be organized so unwastefully that no heavy burden would be laid on the individual citizens; every one of whom as a matter of course would have to pay his toll of some obviously useful work. At present you must note that all the amazing machinery which we have invented has served only to increase the amount of profit-bearing wares; in other words, to increase the amount of profit pouched by individuals for their own advantage, part of which profit they use as capital for the production of more profit, with ever the same waste attached to it; and part as private riches or means for luxurious living, which again is sheer waste—is in fact to be looked on as a kind of bonfire on which rich men burn up the product of the labour they have fleeced from the workers beyond what they themselves can use. So I say that, in spite of our inventions, no worker works under the present system an hour the less on account of those labour-saving machines, so-called. But under a happier state of things they would be used simply for saving labour, with the result of a vast amount of leisure gained for the community to be added to that gained by the avoidance of the waste of useless luxury, and the abolition of the service of commercial war.

And I may say that as to that leisure, as I should in no case do any harm to any one with it, so I should often do some direct good to the community with it, by practising arts or occupations for my hands or brain which would give pleasure to many of the citizens; in other words, a great deal of the best work done would be done in the leisure time of men relieved from any anxiety as to their livelihood, and eager to exercise their special talent, as all men, nay, all animals are.

Now, again, this leisure would enable me to please myself and expand my mind by travelling if I had a mind to it: because, say, for instance, that I were a shoemaker; if due social order were established, it by no means follows that I should always be obliged to make shoes in one place; a due amount of easily conceivable arrangement would enable me to make shoes in Rome, say, for three months, and to come back with new ideas of building, gathered from the sight of the works of past ages, amongst other things which would perhaps be of service in London.

But now, in order that my leisure might not degenerate into idleness and aimlessness, I must set up a claim for due work to do. Nothing to my mind is more important than this demand, and I must ask your leave to say something about it. I have mentioned that I should probably use my leisure for doing a good deal of what is now called work; but it is clear that if I am a member of a Socialist Community I must do my due share of rougher work than this—my due share of what my capacity enables me to do, that is; no fitting of me to a Procrustean bed; but even that share of work necessary to the existence of the simplest social life must, in the first place, whatever else it is, be reasonable work; that is, it must be such work as a good citizen can see the necessity for; as a member of the community, I must have agreed to do it.

To take two strong instances of the contrary, I won't submit to be dressed up in red and marched off to shoot at my French or German or Arab friend in a quarrel that I don't understand; I will rebel sooner than do that.

Nor will I submit to waste my time and energies in making some trifling toy which I know only a fool can desire; I will rebel sooner than do that.

However, you may be sure that in a state of social order I shall have no need to rebel against any such pieces of unreason; only I am forced to speak from the way we live to the way we might live.

Again, if the necessary reasonable work be of a mechanical kind, I must be helped to do it by a machine, not to cheapen my labour, but so that as little time as possible may be spent upon it, and that I may be able to think of other things while am tending the machine. And if the work be specially rough or exhausting, you will, I am sure, agree with me in saying that I must take turns in doing it with other people; I mean I mustn't, for instance, be expected to spend my working hours always at the bottom of a coal-pit. I think such work as that ought to be largely volunteer work, and done, as I say, in spells. And what I say of very rough work I say also of nasty work. On the other hand, I should think very little of the manhood of a stout and healthy man who did not feel a pleasure in doing rough work; always supposing him to work under the conditions I have been speaking of—namely, feeling that it was useful (and consequently honoured), and that it was not continuous or hopeless, and that he was really doing it of his own free will.

The last claim I make for my work is that the places I worked in, factories or workshops, should be pleasant, just as the fields where our most necessary work is done are pleasant. Believe me there is nothing in the world to prevent this being done, save the necessity of making profits on all wares; in other words, the wares are cheapened at the expense of people being forced to work in crowded, unwholesome, squalid, noisy dens: that is to say, they are cheapened at the expense of the workman's life.

Well, so much for my claims as to my necessary work, my tribute to the community. I believe people would find, as they advanced in their capacity for carrying on social order, that life so lived was much less expensive than we now can have any idea of; and that, after a little, people would rather be anxious to seek work than to avoid it; that our working hours would rather be merry parties of men and maids, young men and old enjoying themselves over their work, than the grumpy weariness it mostly is now. Then would come the time for the new birth of art, so much talked of, so long deferred; people could not help showing their mirth and pleasure in their work, and would be always wishing to express it in a tangible and more or less enduring form, and the workshop would once more be a school of art, whose influence no one could escape from.

And, again, that word art leads me to my last claim, which is that the material surroundings of my life should be pleasant, generous, and beautiful; that I know is a large claim, but this I will say about it, that if it cannot be satisfied, if every civilized community cannot provide such surroundings for all its members, I do not want the world to go on; it is a mere misery that man has ever existed. I do not think it possible under the present circumstances to speak too strongly on this point. I feel sure that the time will come when people will find it difficult to believe that a rich community such as ours, having such command over external Nature, could have submitted to live such a mean, shabby, dirty life as we do.

And once for all, there is nothing in our circumstances save the hunting of profit that drives us into it. It is profit which draws men into enormous unmanageable aggregations called towns, for instance; profit which crowds them up when they are there into quarters without gardens or open spaces; profit which won't take the most ordinary precautions against wrapping a whole district in a cloud of sulphurous smoke; which turns beautiful rivers into filthy sewers; which condemns all but the rich to live in houses idiotically cramped and confined at the best, and at the worst in houses for whose wretchedness there is no name.

I say it is almost incredible that we should bear such crass stupidity as this; nor should we if we could help it. We shall not bear it when the workers get out of their heads that they are but an appendage to profit-grinding, that the more profits that are made the more employment at high wages there will be for them, and that therefore all the incredible filth, disorder, and degradation of modern civilization are signs of their prosperity. So far from that, they are signs of their slavery. When they are no longer slaves they will claim as a matter of course that every man and every family should be generously lodged; that every child should be able to play in a garden close to the place his parents live in; that the houses should by their obvious decency and order be ornaments to Nature, not disfigurements of it; for the decency and order above-mentioned when carried to the due pitch would most assuredly lead to beauty in building. All this, of course, would mean the people—that is, all society—duly organized, having in its own hands the means of production, to be owned by no individual, but used by all as occasion called for its use, and can only be done on those terms; on any other terms people will be driven to accumulate private wealth for themselves, and thus, as we have seen, to waste the goods of the community and perpetuate the division into classes, which means continual war and waste.

As to what extent it may be necessary or desirable for people under social order to live in common, we may differ pretty much according to our tendencies towards social life. For my part I can't see why we should think it a hardship to eat with the people we work with; I am sure that as to many things, such as valuable books, pictures, and splendour of surroundings, we shall find it better to club our means together; and I must say that often when I have been sickened by the stupidity of the mean idiotic rabbit warrens that rich men build for themselves in Bayswater and elsewhere, I console myself with visions of the noble communal hall of the future, unsparing of materials, generous in worthy ornament, alive with the noblest thoughts of our time, and the past, embodied in the best art which a free and manly people could produce; such an abode of man as no private enterprise could come anywhere near for beauty and fitness, because only collective thought and collective life could cherish the aspirations which would give birth to its beauty, or have the skill and leisure to carry them out. I for my part should think it much the reverse of a hardship if I had to read my books and meet my friends in such a place; nor do I think I am better off to live in a vulgar stuccoed house crowded with upholstery that I despise, in all respects degrading to the mind and enervating to the body to live in, simply because I call it my own, or my house.

It is not an original remark, but I make it here, that my home is where I meet people with whom I sympathise, whom I love.

Well, that is my opinion as a middle-class man. Whether a working-class man would think his family possession of his wretched little room better than his share of the palace of which I have spoken, I must leave to his opinion, and to the imaginations of the middle class, who perhaps may sometimes conceive the fact that the said worker is cramped for space and comfort—say on washing-day.

Before I leave this matter of the surroundings of life, I wish to meet a possible objection. I have spoken of machinery being used freely for releasing people from the more mechanical and repulsive part of necessary labour; and I know that to some cultivated people, people of the artistic turn of mind, machinery is particularly distasteful, and they will be apt to say you will never get your surroundings pleasant so long as you are surrounded by machinery. I don't quite admit that; it is the allowing machines to be our masters and not our servants that so injures the beauty of life nowadays. In other words, it is the token of the terrible crime we have fallen into of using our control of the powers of Nature for the purpose of enslaving people, we careless meantime of how much happiness we rob their lives of.

Yet for the consolation of the artists I will say that I believe indeed that a state of social order would probably lead at first to a great development of machinery for really useful purposes, because people will still be anxious about getting through the work necessary to holding society together; but that after a while they will find that there is not so much work to do as they expected, and that then they will have leisure to reconsider the whole subject; and if it seems to them that a certain industry would be carried on more pleasantly as regards the worker, and more effectually as regards the goods, by using hand-work rather than machinery, they will certainly get rid of their machinery, because it will be possible for them to do so. It isn't possible now; we are not at liberty to do so; we are slaves to the monsters which we have created. And I have a kind of hope that the very elaboration of machinery in a society whose purpose is not the multiplication of labour, as it now is, but the carrying on of a pleasant life, as it would be under social order—that the elaboration of machinery, I say, will lead the simplification of life, and so once more to the limitation of machinery.

Well, I will now let my claims for decent life stand as I have made them. To sum them up in brief, they are: First, a healthy body; second, an active mind in sympathy with the past, the present, and the future; thirdly, occupation fit for a healthy body and an active mind; and fourthly, a beautiful world to live in.

These are the conditions of life which the refined man of all ages has set before him as the thing above all others to be attained. Too often he has been so foiled in their pursuit that he has turned longing eyes backward to the days before civilization, when man's sole business was getting himself food from day to day, and hope was dormant in him, or at least could not be expressed by him.

Indeed, if civilization (as many think) forbids the realization of the hope to attain such conditions of life, then civilization forbids mankind to be happy; and if that be the case, then let us stifle all aspirations towards progress—nay, all feelings of mutual good-will and affection between men—and snatch each one of us what we can from the heap of wealth that fools create for rogues to grow fat on; or better still, let us as speedily as possible find some means of dying like men, since we are forbidden to live like men.

Rather, however, take courage, and believe that we of this age, in spite of all its torment and disorder, have been born to a wonderful heritage fashioned of the work of those that have gone before us; and that the day of the organization of man is dawning. It is not we who can build up the new social order; the past ages have done the most of that work for us; but we can clear our eyes to the signs of the times, and we shall then see that the attainment of a good condition of life is being made possible for us, and that it is now our business to stretch out our hands to take it.

And how? Chiefly, I think, by educating people to a sense of their real capacities as men, so that they may be able to use to their own good the political power which is rapidly being thrust upon them; to get them to see that the old system of organizing labour for individual profit is becoming unmanageable, and that the whole people have now got to choose between the confusion resulting from the break up of that system and the determination to take in hand the labour now organized for profit, and use its organization for the livelihood of the community: to get people to see that individual profit-makers are not a necessity for labour but an obstruction to it, and that not only or chiefly because they are the perpetual pensioners of labour, as they are, but rather because of the waste which their existence as a class necessitates. All this we have to teach people, when we have taught ourselves; and I admit that the work is long and burdensome; as I began by saying, people have been made so timorous of change by the terror of starvation that even the unluckiest of them are stolid and hard to move. Hard as the work is, however, its reward is not doubtful. The mere fact that a body of men, however small, are banded together as Socialist missionaries shows that the change is going on. As the working-classes, the real organic part of society, take in these ideas, hope will arise in them, and they will claim changes in society, many of which doubtless will not tend directly towards their emancipation, because they will be claimed without due knowledge of the one thing necessary to claim, equality of condition; but which indirectly will help to break up our rotten sham society, while that claim for equality of condition will be made constantly and with growing loudness till it must be listened to, and then at last it will only be a step over the border and the civilized world will be socialized; and, looking back on what has been, we shall be astonished to think of how long we submitted to live as we live now.

WHIGS, DEMOCRATS, AND SOCIALISTS. [37a]

What is the state of parties in England to-day? How shall we enumerate them? The Whigs, who stand first on the list in my title, are considered generally to be the survival of an old historical party once looked on as having democratic tendencies, but now the hope of all who would stand soberly on the ancient ways. Besides these, there are Tories also, the descendants of the stout defenders of Church and State and the divine right of kings.

Now, I don't mean to say but that at the back of this ancient name of Tory there lies a great mass of genuine Conservative feeling, held by people who, if they had their own way, would play some rather fantastic tricks, I fancy; nay, even might in the course of time be somewhat rough with such people as are in this hall at present. [37b] But this feeling, after all, is only a sentiment now; all practical hope has died out of it, and these worthy people cannot have their own way. It is true that they elect members of Parliament, who talk very big to please them, and sometimes even they manage to get a Government into power that nominally represents their sentiment, but when that happens the said Government is forced, even when its party has a majority in the House of Commons, to take a much lower standpoint than the high Tory ideal; the utmost that the real Tory party can do, even when backed by the Primrose League and its sham hierarchy, is to delude the electors to return Tories to Parliament to pass measures more akin to Radicalism than the Whigs durst attempt, so that, though there are Tories, there is no Tory party in England.

On the other hand, there is a party, which I can call for the present by no other name than Whig, which is both numerous and very powerful, and which does, in fact, govern England, and to my mind will always do so as long as the present constitutional Parliament lasts. Of course, like all parties it includes men of various shades of opinion, from the Tory-tinted Whiggery of Lord Salisbury to the Radical-tinted Whiggery of Mr. Chamberlain's present tail. Neither do I mean to say that they are conscious of being a united party; on the contrary, the groups will sometimes oppose each other furiously at elections, and perhaps the more simple-minded of them really think that it is a matter of importance to the nation which section of them may be in power; but they may always be reckoned upon to be in their places and vote against any measure which carries with it a real attack on our constitutional system; surely very naturally, since they are there for no other purpose than to do so. They are, and always must be, conscious defenders of the present system, political and economical, as long as they have any cohesion as Tories, Whigs, Liberals, or even Radicals. Not one of them probably would go such a very short journey towards revolution as the abolition of the House of Lords. A one-chamber Parliament would seem to them an impious horror, and the abolition of the monarchy they would consider a serious inconvenience to the London tradesman.

Now this is the real Parliamentary Party, at present divided into jarring sections under the influence of the survival of the party warfare of the last few generations, but which already shows signs of sinking its differences so as to offer a solid front of resistance to the growing instinct which on its side will before long result in a party claiming full economical as well as political freedom for the whole people.

But is there nothing in Parliament, or seeking entrance to it, except this variously tinted Whiggery, this Harlequin of Reaction? Well, inside Parliament, setting aside the Irish party, which is, we may now well hope, merely temporarily there, there is not much. It is not among people of "wealth and local influence," who I see are supposed to be the only available candidates for Parliament of a recognized party, that you will find the elements of revolution. We will grant that there are some few genuine Democrats there, and let them pass. But outside there are undoubtedly many who are genuine Democrats, and who have it in their heads that it is both possible and desirable to capture the constitutional Parliament and turn it into a real popular assembly, which, with the people behind it, might lead us peaceably and constitutionally into the great Revolution which all thoughtful men desire to bring about; all thoughtful men, that is, who do not belong to the consciously cynical Tories, i.e., men determined, whether it be just or unjust, good for humanity or bad for it, to keep the people down as long as they can, which they hope, very naturally, will be as long as they live.

To capture Parliament and turn it into a popular but constitutional assembly is, I must conclude, the aspiration of the genuine Democrats wherever they may be found; that is their idea of the first step of the Democratic policy. The questions to be asked of this, as of all other policies, are first, What is the end proposed by it? and secondly, Are they likely to succeed? As to the end proposed, I think there is much difference of opinion. Some Democrats would answer from the merely political point of view, and say: Universal suffrage, payment of members, annual Parliaments, abolition of the House of Lords, abolition of the monarchy, and so forth. I would answer this by saying: After all, these are not ends, but means to an end; and passing by the fact that the last two are not constitutional measures, and so could not be brought about without actual rebellion, I would say if you had gained all these things, and more, all you would have done would have been to establish the ascendancy of the Democratic party; having so established it, you would then have to find out by the usual party means what that Democratic party meant, and you would find that your triumph in mere politics would lead you back again exactly to the place you started from. You would be Whigs under a different name. Monarchy, House of Lords, pensions, standing army, and the rest of it, are only supports to the present social system—the privilege based on the wages and capital system of production—and are worth nothing except as supports to it. If you are determined to support that system, therefore, you had better leave these things alone. The real masters of Society, the real tyrants of the people, are the Landlords and Capitalists, whom your political triumph would not interfere with.

Then, as now, there would be a proletariat and a moneyed class. Then, as now, it would be possible sometimes for a diligent, energetic man, with his mind set wholly on such success, to climb out of the proletariat into the moneyed class, there to sweat as he once was sweated; which, my friends, is, if you will excuse the word, your ridiculous idea of freedom of contract.

The sole and utmost success of your policy would be that it might raise up a strong opposition to the condition of things which it would be your function to uphold; but most probably such opposition would still be outside Parliament, and not in it; you would have made a revolution, probably not without bloodshed, only to show people the necessity for another revolution the very next day.

Will you think the example of America too trite? Anyhow, consider it! A country with universal suffrage, no king, no House of Lords, no privilege as you fondly think; only a little standing army, chiefly used for the murder of red-skins; a democracy after your model; and with all that, a society corrupt to the core, and at this moment engaged in suppressing freedom with just the same reckless brutality and blind ignorance as the Czar of all the Russias uses. [43]

But it will be said, and certainly with much truth, that not all the Democrats are for mere political reform. I say that I believe that this is true, and it is a very important truth too. I will go farther, and will say that all those Democrats who can be distinguished from Whigs do intend social reforms which they hope will somewhat alter the relations of the classes towards each other; and there is, generally speaking, amongst Democrats a leaning towards a kind of limited State-Socialism, and it is through that that they hope to bring about a peaceful revolution, which, if it does not introduce a condition of equality, will at least make the workers better off and contented with their lot.

They hope to get a body of representatives elected to Parliament, and by them to get measure after measure passed which will tend towards this goal; nor would some of them, perhaps most of them, be discontented if by this means we could glide into complete State-Socialism. I think that the present Democrats are widely tinged with this idea, and to me it is a matter of hope that it is so; whatever of error there is in it, it means advance beyond the complete barrenness of the mere political programme.

Yet I must point out to these semi-Socialist Democrats that in the first place they will be made the cat's-paw of some of the wilier of the Whigs. There are several of these measures which look to some Socialistic, as, for instance, the allotments scheme, and other schemes tending toward peasant proprietorship, co-operation, and the like, but which after all, in spite of their benevolent appearance, are really weapons in the hands of reactionaries, having for their real object the creation of a new middle-class made out of the working-class and at their expense; the raising, in short, of a new army against the attack of the disinherited.

There is no end to this kind of dodge, nor will be apparently till there is an end of the class which tries it on; and a great many of the Democrats will be amused and absorbed by it from time to time. They call this sort of nonsense "practical;" it seems like doing something, while the steady propaganda of a principle which must prevail in the end is, according to them, doing nothing, and is unpractical. For the rest, it is not likely to become dangerous, further than as it clogs the wheels of the real movement somewhat, because it is sometimes a mere piece of reaction, as when, for instance, it takes the form of peasant proprietorship, flying right in the face of the commercial development of the day, which tends ever more and more towards the aggregation of capital, thereby smoothing the way for the organized possession of the means of production by the workers when the true revolution shall come: while, on the other hand, when this attempt to manufacture a new middle-class takes the form of co-operation and the like, it is not dangerous, because it means nothing more than a slightly altered form of joint-stockery, and everybody almost is beginning to see this. The greed of men stimulated by the spectacle of profit-making all around them, and also by the burden of the interest on the money which they have been obliged to borrow, will not allow them even to approach a true system of co-operation. Those benefited by the transaction presently become eager shareholders in a commercial speculation, and if they are working-men, as they often are, they are also capitalists. The enormous commercial success of the great co-operative societies, and the absolute no-effect of that success on the social conditions of the workers, are sufficient tokens of what this non-political co-operation must come to: "Nothing—it shall not be less."

But again, it may be said, some of the Democrats go farther than this; they take up actual pieces of Socialism, and are more than inclined to support them. Nationalization of the land, or of railways, or cumulative taxation on incomes, or limiting the right of inheritance, or new factory laws, or the restriction by law of the day's labour—one of these, or more than one sometimes, the Democrats will support, and see absolute salvation in these one or two planks of the platform. All this I admit, and once again say it is a hopeful sign, and yet once again I say there is a snare in it—a snake lies lurking in the grass.

Those who think that they can deal with our present system in this piecemeal way very much underrate the strength of the tremendous organization under which we live, and which appoints to each of us his place, and if we do not chance to fit it, grinds us down till we do. Nothing but a tremendous force can deal with this force; it will not suffer itself to be dismembered, nor to lose anything which really is its essence without putting forth all its force in resistance; rather than lose anything which it considers of importance, it will pull the roof of the world down upon its head. For, indeed, I grant these semi-Socialist Democrats that there is one hope for their tampering piecemeal with our Society; if by chance they can excite people into seriously, however blindly, claiming one or other of these things in question, and could be successful in Parliament in driving it through, they would certainly draw on a great civil war, and such a war once let loose would not end but either with the full triumph of Socialism or its extinction for the present; it would be impossible to limit the aim of the struggle; nor can we even guess at the course which it would take, except that it could not be a matter of compromise. But suppose the Democratic party peaceably successful on this new basis of semi-State Socialism, what would it all mean? Attempts to balance the two classes whose interests are opposed to each other, a mere ignoring of this antagonism which has led us through so many centuries to where we are now, and then, after a period of disappointment and disaster, the naked conflict once more; a revolution made, and another immediately necessary on its morrow!

Yet, indeed, it will not come to that; for, whatever may be the aims of the Democrats, they will not succeed in getting themselves into a position from whence they could make the attempt to realize them. I have said there are Tories and yet no real Tory party; so also it seems to me that there are Democrats but no Democratic party; at present they are used by the leaders of the parliamentary factions, and also kept at a distance by them from any real power. If they by hook or crook managed to get a number of members into Parliament, they would find out their differences very speedily under the influence of party rule; in point of fact, the Democrats are not a party; because they have no principles other than the old Whig Radical ones, extended in some cases so as to take in a little semi-Socialism which the march of events has forced on them—that is, they gravitate on one side to the Whigs and on the other to the Socialists. Whenever, if ever, they begin to be a power in the elections and get members in the House, the temptation to be members of a real live party which may have the government of the country in its hands, the temptation to what is (facetiously, I suppose) called practical politics, will be too much for many, even of those who gravitate towards Socialism; a quasi-Democratic parliamentary party, therefore, would probably be merely a recruiting ground, a nursery for the left wing of the Whigs; though it would indeed leave behind some small nucleus of opposition, the principles of which, however, would be vague and floating, so that it would be but a powerless group after all.

The future of the constitutional Parliament, therefore, it seems to me, is a perpetual Whig Rump, which will yield to pressure when mere political reforms are attempted to be got out of it, but will be quite immovable towards any real change in social and economical matters; that is to say, so far as it may be conscious of the attack; for I grant that it may be betrayed into passing semi-State-Socialistic measures, which will do this amount of good, that they will help to entangle commerce in difficulties, and so add to discontent by creating suffering; suffering of which the people will not understand the causes definitely, but which their instinct will tell them truly is brought about by government, and that, too, the only kind of government which they can have so long as the constitutional Parliament lasts.

Now, if you think I have exaggerated the power of the Whigs, that is, of solid, dead, unmoving resistance to progress, I must call your attention to the events of the last few weeks. Here has been a measure of pacification proposed; at the least and worst an attempt to enter upon a pacification of a weary and miserable quarrel many centuries old. The British people, in spite of their hereditary prejudice against the Irish, were not averse to the measure; the Tories were, as usual, powerless against it; yet so strong has been the vis inertiæ of Whiggery that it has won a notable victory over common-sense and sentiment combined, and has drawn over to it a section of those hitherto known as Radicals, and probably would have drawn all Radicals over but for the personal ascendancy of Mr. Gladstone. The Whigs, seeing, if but dimly, that this Irish Independence meant an attack on property, have been successful in snatching the promised peace out of the people's hands, and in preparing all kinds of entanglement and confusion for us for a long while in their steady resistance to even the beginnings of revolution.

This, therefore, is what Parliament looks to me: a solid central party, with mere nebulous opposition on the right hand and on the left. The people governed; that is to say, fair play amongst themselves for the money-privileged classes to make the most of their privilege, and to fight sturdily with each other in doing so; but the government concealed as much as possible, and also as long as possible; that is to say, the government resting on an assumed necessary eternity of privilege to monopolize the means of the fructification of labour.

For so long as that assumption is accepted by the ignorance of the people, the Great Whig Rump will remain inexpugnable, but as soon as the people's eyes are opened, even partially—and they begin to understand the meaning of the words, the Emancipation of Labour—we shall begin to have an assured hope of throwing off the basest and most sordid tyranny which the world has yet seen, the tyranny of so-called Constitutionalism.

How, then, are the people's eyes to be opened? By the force evolved from the final triumph and consequent corruption of Commercial Whiggery, which force will include in it a recognition of its constructive activity by intelligent people on the one hand, and on the other half-blind instinctive struggles to use its destructive activity on the part of those who suffer and have not been allowed to think; and, to boot, a great deal that goes between those two extremes.

In this turmoil, all those who can be truly called Socialists will be involved. The modern development of the great class-struggle has forced us to think, our thoughts force us to speak, and our hopes force us to try to get a hearing from the people. Nor can one tell how far our words will carry, so to say. The most moderate exposition of our principles will bear with it the seeds of disruption; nor can we tell what form that disruption will take.

One and all, then, we are responsible for the enunciation of Socialist principles and of the consequences which may flow from their general acceptance, whatever that may be. This responsibility no Socialist can shake off by declarations against physical force and in favour of constitutional methods of agitation; we are attacking the Constitution with the very beginnings, the mere lispings, of Socialism.

Whiggery, therefore, in its various forms, is the representative of Constitutionalism—is the outward expression of monopoly and consequent artificial restraints on labour and life; and there is only one expression of the force which will destroy Whiggery, and that is Socialism; and on the right hand and on the left Toryism and Radicalism will melt into Whiggery—are doing so now—and Socialism has got to absorb all that is not Whig in Radicalism.

Then comes the question, What is the policy of Socialism? If Toryism and Democracy are only nebulous masses of opposition to the solid centre of Whiggery, what can we call Socialism?

Well, at present, in England at least, Socialism is not a party, but a sect. That is sometimes brought against it as a taunt; but I am not dismayed by it; for I can conceive of a sect—nay, I have heard of one—becoming a very formidable power, and becoming so by dint of its long remaining a sect. So I think it is quite possible that Socialism will remain a sect till the very eve of the last stroke that completes the revolution, after which it will melt into the new Society. And is it not sects, bodies of definite, uncompromising principles, that lead us into revolutions? Was it not so in the Cromwellian times? Nay, have not the Fenian sect, even in our own days, made Home Rule possible? They may give birth to parties, though not parties themselves. And what should a sect like we are have to do in the parliamentary struggle—we who have an ideal to keep always before ourselves and others, and who cannot accept compromise; who can see nothing that can give us rest for a minute save the emancipation of labour, which will be brought about by the workers gaining possession of all the means of the fructification of labour; and who, even when that is gained, shall have pure Communism ahead to strive for?

What are we to do, then? Stand by and look on? Not exactly. Yet we may look on other people doing their work while we do ours. They are already beginning, as I have said, to stumble about with attempts at State Socialism. Let them make their experiments and blunders, and prepare the way for us by so doing. And our own business? Well, we—sect or party, or group of self-seekers, madmen, and poets, which you will—are at least the only set of people who have been able to see that there is and has been a great class-struggle going on. Further, we can see that this class-struggle cannot come to an end till the classes themselves do: one class must absorb the other. Which, then? Surely the useful one, the one that the world lives by, and on. The business of the people at present is to make it impossible for the useless, non-producing class to live; while the business of Constitutionalism is, on the contrary, to make it possible for them to live. And our business is to help to make the people conscious of this great antagonism between the people and Constitutionalism; and meantime to let Constitutionalism go on with its government unhelped by us at least, until it at last becomes conscious of its burden of the people's hate, of the people's knowledge that it is disinherited, which we shall have done our best to further by any means that we could.

As to Socialists in Parliament, there are two words about that. If they go there to take a part in carrying on Constitutionalism by palliating the evils of the system, and so helping our rulers to bear their burden of government, I for one, and so far as their action therein goes, cannot call them Socialists at all. But if they go there with the intention of doing what they can towards the disruption of Parliament, that is a matter of tactics for the time being; but even here I cannot help seeing the danger of their being seduced from their true errand, and I fear that they might become, on the terms above mentioned, simply supporters of the very thing they set out to undo.

I say that our work lies quite outside Parliament, and it is to help to educate the people by every and any means that may be effective; and the knowledge we have to help them to is threefold—to know their own, to know how to take their own, and to know how to use their own.

FEUDAL ENGLAND.

It is true that the Norman Conquest found a certain kind of feudality in existence in England—a feudality which was developed from the customs of the Teutonic tribes with no admixture of Roman law; and also that even before the Conquest this country was slowly beginning to be mixed up with the affairs of the Continent of Europe, and that not only with the kindred nations of Scandinavia, but with the Romanized countries also. But the Conquest of Duke William did introduce the complete Feudal system into the country; and it also connected it by strong bonds to the Romanized countries, and yet by so doing laid the first foundations of national feeling in England. The English felt their kinship with the Norsemen or the Danes, and did not suffer from their conquests when they had become complete, and when, consequently, mere immediate violence had disappeared from them; their feeling was tribal rather than national; but they could have no sense of tribal unity with the varied populations of the provinces which mere dynastical events had strung together into the dominion, the manor, one may say, of the foreign princes of Normandy and Anjou; and, as the kings who ruled them gradually got pushed out of their French possessions, England began to struggle against the domination of men felt to be foreigners, and so gradually became conscious of her separate nationality, though still only in a fashion, as the manor of an English lord.

It is beyond the scope of this piece to give anything like a connected story, even of the slightest, of the course of events between the conquest of Duke William and the fully developed mediæval period of the fourteenth century, which is the England that I have before my eyes as Mediæval or Feudal. That period of the fourteenth century united the developments of the elements which had been stirring in Europe since the final fall of the Roman Empire, and England shared in the general feeling and spirit of the age, although, from its position, the course of its history, and to a certain extent the lives of its people, were different. It is to this period, therefore, that I wish in the long run to call your attention, and I will only say so much about the earlier period as may be necessary to explain how the people of England got into the position in which they were found by the Statute of Labourers enacted by Edward III., and the Peasants' Rebellion in the time of his grandson and successor, Richard II.

Undoubtedly, then, the Norman Conquest made a complete break in the continuity of the history of England. When the Londoners after the Battle of Hastings accepted Duke William for their king, no doubt they thought of him as occupying much the same position as that of the newly slain Harold; or at any rate they looked on him as being such a king of England as Knut the Dane, who had also conquered the country; and probably William himself thought no otherwise; but the event was quite different; for on the one hand, not only was he a man of strong character, able, masterful, and a great soldier in the modern sense of the word, but he had at his back his wealthy dukedom of Normandy, which he had himself reduced to obedience and organized; and, on the other hand, England lay before him, unorganized, yet stubbornly rebellious to him; its very disorganization and want of a centre making it more difficult to deal with by merely overrunning it with an army levied for that purpose, and backed by a body of house-carles or guards, which would have been the method of a Scandinavian or native king in dealing with his rebellious subjects. Duke William's necessities and instincts combined led him into a very different course of action, which determined the future destiny of the country. What he did was to quarter upon England an army of feudal vassals drawn from his obedient dukedom, and to hand over to them the lordship of the land of England in return for their military service to him, the suzerain of them all. Thenceforward, it was under the rule of these foreign landlords that the people of England had to develop.

The development of the country as a Teutonic people was checked and turned aside by this event. Duke William brought, in fact, his Normandy into England, which was thereby changed from a Teutonic people (Old-Norse theod), with the tribal customary law still in use among them, into a province of Romanized Feudal Europe, a piece of France, in short; and though in time she did grow into another England again, she missed for ever in her laws, and still more in her language and her literature, the chance of developing into a great homogeneous Teutonic people infused usefully with a mixture of Celtic blood.

However, this step which Duke William was forced to take further influenced the future of the country by creating the great order of the Baronage, and the history of the early period of England is pretty much that of the struggle of the king with the Baronage and the Church. For William fixed the type of the successful English mediæval king, of whom Henry II. and Edward I. were the most notable examples afterwards. It was, in fact, with him that the struggle towards monarchical bureaucracy began, which was checked by the barons, who extorted Magna Charta from King John, and afterwards by the revolt headed by Simon de Montfort in Henry III.'s reign; was carried on vigorously by Edward I., and finally successfully finished by Henry VII. after the long faction-fight of the Wars of the Roses had weakened the feudal lords so much that they could no longer assert themselves against the monarchy.

As to the other political struggle of the Middle Ages, the contest between the Crown and the Church, two things are to be noted; first, that at least in the earlier period the Church was on the popular side. Thomas Beckett was canonized, it is true, formally and by regular decree; but his memory was held so dear by the people that he would probably have been canonized informally by them if the holy seat at Rome had refused to do so. The second thing to be noted about the dispute is this, that it was no contest of principle. According to the mediæval theory of life and religion, the Church and the State were one in essence, and but separate manifestations of the Kingdom of God upon earth, which was part of the Kingdom of God in heaven. The king was an officer of that realm and a liegeman of God. The doctor of laws and the doctor of physic partook in a degree of the priestly character. On the other hand, the Church was not withdrawn from the every-day life of men; the division into a worldly and spiritual life, neither of which had much to do with the other, was a creation of the protestantism of the Reformation, and had no place in the practice at least of the mediæval Church, which we cannot too carefully remember is little more represented by modern Catholicism than by modern Protestantism. The contest, therefore, between the Crown and the Church was a mere bickering between two bodies, without any essential antagonism between them, as to how far the administration of either reached; neither dreamed of subordinating one to the other, far less of extinguishing one by the other.

The history of the Crusades, by-the-way, illustrates very emphatically this position of the Church in the Middle Ages. The foundation of that strange feudal kingdom of Jerusalem, whose very coat of arms was a solecism in heraldry, whose king had precedence, in virtue of his place as lord of the centre of Christianity, over all other kings and princes; the orders of men-at-arms vowed to poverty and chastity, like the Templars and Knights of St. John; and above all the unquestioning sense of duty that urged men of all classes and kinds into the holy war, show how strongly the idea of God's Kingdom on the earth had taken hold of all men's minds in the early Middle Ages. As to the result of the Crusades, they certainly had their influence on the solidification of Europe and the great feudal system, at the head of which, in theory at least, were the Pope and the Kaiser. For the rest, the intercourse with the East gave Europe an opportunity of sharing in the mechanical civilization of the peoples originally dominated by the Arabs, and infused by the art of Byzantium and Persia, not without some tincture of the cultivation of the latter classical period.

The stir and movement also of the Crusades, and the necessities in which they involved the princes and their barons, furthered the upward movement of the classes that lay below the feudal vassals, great and little; the principal opportunity for which movement, however, in England, was given by the continuous struggle between the Crown and the Church and Baronage.

The early Norman kings, even immediately after the death of the Conqueror, found themselves involved in this struggle, and were forced to avail themselves of the help of what had now become the inferior tribe—the native English, to wit. Henry I., an able and ambitious man, understood this so clearly that he made a distinct bid for the favour of the inferior tribe by marrying an English princess; and it was by means of the help of his English subjects that he conquered his Norman subjects, and the field of Tenchebray, which put the coping-stone on his success, was felt by the English people as an English victory over the oppressing tribe with which Duke William had overwhelmed the English people. It was during this king's reign and under these influences that the trading and industrial classes began to rise somewhat. The merchant gilds were now in their period of greatest power, and had but just begun, in England at least, to develop into the corporations of the towns; but the towns themselves were beginning to gain their freedom and to become an important element in the society of the time, as little by little they asserted themselves against the arbitrary rule of the feudal lords, lay or ecclesiastical: for as to the latter, it must be remembered that the Church included in herself the orders or classes into which lay society was divided, and while by its lower clergy of the parishes and by the friars it touched the people, its upper clergy were simply feudal lords; and as the religious fervour of the higher clergy, which was marked enough in the earlier period of the Middle Ages (in Anselm, for example), faded out, they became more and more mere landlords, although from the conditions of their landlordism, living as they did on their land and amidst of their tenants, they were less oppressive than the lay landlords.

The order and progress of Henry I.'s reign, which marks the transition from the mere military camp of the Conqueror to the mediæval England I have to dwell upon, was followed by the period of mere confusion and misery which accompanied the accession of the princes of Anjou to the throne of England. In this period the barons widely became mere violent and illegal robbers; and the castles with which the land was dotted, and which were begun under the auspices of the Conqueror as military posts, became mere dens of strong-thieves.

No doubt this made the business of the next able king, Henry II., the easier. He was a staunch man of business, and turned himself with his whole soul towards the establishment of order and the consolidation of the monarchy, which accordingly took a great stride under him towards its ultimate goal of bureaucracy. He would probably have carried the business still farther, since in his contest with the Church, in spite of the canonization of Beckett and the king's formal penance at his tomb, he had in fact gained a victory for the Crown which it never really lost again; but in his days England was only a part of the vast dominion of his House, which included more than half of France, and his struggle with his feudatories and the French king, which sowed the seed of the loss of that dominion to the English Crown, took up much of his life, and finally beat him.

His two immediate successors, Richard I. and John, were good specimens of the chiefs of their line, almost all of whom were very able men, having even a touch of genius in them, but therewithal were such wanton blackguards and scoundrels that one is almost forced to apply the theological word "wickedness" to them. Such characters belong specially to their times, fertile as they were both of great qualities and of scoundrelism, and in which our own special vice of hypocrisy was entirely lacking. John, the second of these two pests, put the coping-stone on the villany of his family, and lost his French dominion in the lump.

Under such rascals as these came the turn of the Baronage; and they, led by Stephen Langton, the archbishop who had been thrust on the unwilling king by the Pope, united together and forced from him his assent to Magna Charta, the great, thoroughly well-considered deed, which is conventionally called the foundation of English Liberty, but which can only claim to be so on the ground that it was the confirmation and seal of the complete feudal system in England, and put the relations between the vassals, the great feudatories, and the king on a stable basis; since it created, or at least confirmed, order among these privileged classes, among whom, indeed, it recognized the towns to a certain extent as part of the great feudal hierarchy: so that even by this time they had begun to acquire status in that hierarchy.

So John passed away, and became not long after an almost mythical personage, the type of the bad king. There are still ballads, and prose stories deduced from these ballads, in existence, which tell the tale of this strange monster as the English people imagined it.

As they belong to the literature of the fourteenth century, the period I have undertaken to tell you about specially, I will give you one of the latter of these concerning the death of King John, for whom the people imagined a more dramatic cause of death than mere indigestion, of which in all probability he really died; and you may take it for a specimen of popular literature of the fourteenth century.

I can here make bold to quote from memory, without departing very widely from the old text, since the quaint wording of the original, and the spirit of bold and blunt heroism which it breathes, have fixed it in my mind for ever.

The king, you must remember, had halted at Swinestead Abbey, in Lincolnshire, in his retreat from the hostile barons and their French allies, and had lost all his baggage by the surprise of the advancing tide in the Wash; so that he might well be in a somewhat sour mood.

Says the tale: So the king went to meat in the hall, and before him was a loaf; and he looked grimly on it and said, 'For how much is such a loaf sold in this realm?'

'Sir, for one penny,' said they.

Then the king smote the board with his fist and said, 'By God, if I live for one year such a loaf shall be sold for twelve pence!'

That heard one of the monks who stood thereby, and he thought and considered that his hour and time to die was come, and that it would be a good deed to slay so cruel a king and so evil a lord.

So he went into the garden and plucked plums and took out of them the steles [stalks], and did venom in them each one; and he came before the king and sat on his knee, and said:

'Sir, by St. Austin, this is fruit of our garden.'

Then the king looked evilly on him and said, 'Assay them, monk!'

So the monk took and ate thereof, nor changed countenance any whit: and the king ate thereafter.

But presently afterwards the monk swelled and turned blue, and fell down and died before the king: then waxed the king sick at heart, and he also swelled and died, and so he ended his days.

For a while after the death of John and the accession of Henry III. the Baronage, strengthened by the great Charter and with a weak and wayward king on the throne, made their step forward in power and popularity, and the first serious check to the tendency to monarchical bureaucracy, a kind of elementary aristocratic constitution, was imposed upon the weakness of Henry III. Under this movement of the barons, who in their turn had to seek for the support of the people, the towns made a fresh step in advance, and Simon de Montfort, the leader of what for want of a better word must be called the popular party, was forced by his circumstances to summon to his Parliament citizens from the boroughs. Earl Simon was one of those men that come to the front in violent times, and he added real nobility of character to strength of will and persistence. He became the hero of the people, who went near to canonizing him after his death. But the monarchy was too strong for him and his really advanced projects, which by no means squared with the hopes of the Baronage in general: and when Prince Edward, afterwards Edward I., grown to his full mental stature, came to the help of the Crown with his unscrupulous business ability, the struggle was soon over; and with Evesham field the monarchy began to take a new stride, and the longest yet taken, towards bureaucracy.

Edward I. is remembered by us chiefly for the struggle he carried on with the Scotch Baronage for the feudal suzerainty of that kingdom, and the centuries of animosity between the two countries which that struggle drew on. But he has other claims to our attention besides this.

At first, and remembering the ruthlessness of many of his acts, especially in the Scotch war, one is apt to look upon him as a somewhat pedantic tyrant and a good soldier, with something like a dash of hypocrisy beyond his time added. But, like the Angevine kings I was speaking of just now, he was a completely characteristic product of his time. He was not a hypocrite probably, after all, in spite of his tears shed after he had irretrievably lost a game, or after he had won one by stern cruelty. There was a dash of real romance in him, which mingled curiously with his lawyer-like qualities. He was, perhaps, the man of all men who represented most completely the finished feudal system, and who took it most to heart. His law, his romance, and his religion, his self-command, and his terrible fury were all a part of this innate feudalism, and exercised within its limits; and we must suppose that he thoroughly felt his responsibility as the chief of his feudatories, while at the same time he had no idea of his having any responsibilities towards the lower part of his subjects. Such a man was specially suited to carrying on the tendency to bureaucratic centralization, which culminated in the Tudor monarchy. He had his struggle with the Baronage, but hard as it was, he was sure not to carry it beyond the due limits of feudalism; to that he was always loyal. He had slain Earl Simon before he was king, while he was but his father's general; but Earl Simon's work did not die with him, and henceforward, while the Middle Ages and their feudal hierarchy lasted, it was impossible for either king or barons to do anything which would seriously injure each other's position; the struggle ended in his reign in a balance of power in England which, on the one hand, prevented any great feudatory becoming a rival of the king, as happened in several instances in France, and on the other hand prevented the king lapsing into a mere despotic monarch.

I have said that bureaucracy took a great stride in Edward's reign, but it reached its limits under feudalism as far as the nobles were concerned. Peace and order was established between the different powers of the governing classes; henceforward, the struggle is between them and the governed; that struggle was now to become obvious; the lower tribe was rising in importance; it was becoming richer for fleecing, but also it was beginning to have some power; this led the king first, and afterwards the barons, to attack it definitely; it was rich enough to pay for the trouble of being robbed, and not yet strong enough to defend itself with open success, although the slower and less showy success of growth did not fail it. The instrument of attack in the hands of the barons was the ordinary feudal privilege, the logical carrying out of serfdom; but this attack took place two reigns later. We shall come to that further on. The attack on the lower tribe which was now growing into importance was in this reign made by the king; and his instrument was—Parliament.

I have told you that Simon de Montfort made some attempt to get the burgesses to sit in his Parliament, but it was left to Edward I. to lay the foundations firmly of parliamentary representation, which he used for the purpose of augmenting the power of the Crown and crushing the rising liberty of the towns, though of course his direct aim was simply at—money.

The Great Council of the Realm was purely feudal; it was composed of the feudatories of the king, theoretically of all of them, practically of the great ones only. It was, in fact, the council of the conquering tribe with their chief at its head; the matters of the due feudal tribute, aids, reliefs, fines, scutage, and the like—in short, the king's revenue due from his men—were settled in this council at once and in the lump. But the inferior tribe, though not represented there, existed, and, as aforesaid, was growing rich, and the king had to get their money out of their purses directly; which, as they were not represented at the council, he had to do by means of his officers (the sheriffs) dealing with them one after another, which was a troublesome job; for the men were stiff-necked and quite disinclined to part with their money; and the robbery having to be done on the spot, so to say, encountered all sorts of opposition: and, in fact, it was the money needs both of baron, bishop, and king which had been the chief instrument in furthering the progress of the towns. The towns would be pressed by their lords, king, or baron, or bishop, as it might be, and they would see their advantage and strike a bargain. For you are not to imagine that because there was a deal of violence going on in those times there was no respect for law; on the contrary, there was a quite exaggerated respect for it if it came within the four corners of the feudal feeling, and the result of this feeling of respect was the constant struggle for status on the part of the townships and other associations throughout the Middle Ages.

Well, the burghers would say, "'Tis hard to pay this money, but we will put ourselves out to pay it if you will do something for us in return; let, for example, our men be tried in our own court, and the verdict be of one of compurgation instead of wager of battle," and so forth, and so forth.

All this sort of detailed bargaining was, in fact, a safeguard for the local liberties, so far as they went, of the towns and shires, and did not suit the king's views of law and order at all; and so began the custom of the sheriff (the king's officer, who had taken the place of the earl of the Anglo-Saxon period) summoning the burgesses to the council, which burgesses you must understand were not elected at the folkmotes of the town, or hundred, but in a sort of hole-and-corner way by a few of the bigger men of the place. What the king practically said was this: "I want your money, and I cannot be for ever wrangling with you stubborn churles at home there, and listening to all your stories of how poor you are, and what you want; no, I want you to be represented. Send me up from each one of your communes a man or two whom I can bully or cajole or bribe to sign away your substance for you."

Under these circumstances it is no wonder that the towns were not very eager in the cause of representation. It was no easy job to get them to come up to London merely to consult as to the kind of sauce with which they were to be eaten. However, they did come in some numbers, and by the year 1295 something like a shadow of our present Parliament was on foot. Nor need there be much more said about this institution; as time went on its functions got gradually extended by the petition for the redress of grievances accompanying the granting of money, but it was generally to be reckoned on as subservient to the will of the king, who down to the later Tudor period played some very queer tunes on this constitutional instrument.

Edward I. gave place to his son, who again was of the type of king who had hitherto given the opportunity to the barons for their turn of advancement in the constitutional struggle; and in earlier times no doubt they would have taken full advantage of the circumstances; as it was they had little to gain. The king did his best to throw off the restraint of the feudal constitution, and to govern simply as an absolute monarch. After a time of apparent success he failed, of course, and only succeeded in confirming the legal rights of feudalism by bringing about his own formal deposition at the hands of the Baronage, as a chief who, having broken the compact with his feudatories, had necessarily forfeited his right. If we compare his case with that of Charles I. we shall find this difference in it, besides the obvious one that Edward was held responsible to his feudatories and Charles towards the upper middle classes, the squirearchy, as represented by Parliament; that Charles was condemned by a law created for the purpose, so to say, and evolved from the principle of the representation of the propertied classes, while Edward's deposition was the real logical outcome of the confirmed feudal system, and was practically legal and regular.

The successor of the deposed king, the third Edward, ushers in the complete and central period of the Middle Ages in England. The feudal system is complete: the life and spirit of the country has developed into a condition if not quite independent, yet quite forgetful, on the one hand of the ideas and customs of the Celtic and Teutonic tribes, and on the other of the authority of the Roman Empire. The Middle Ages have grown into manhood; that manhood has an art of its own, which, though developed step by step from that of Old Rome and New Rome, and embracing the strange mysticism and dreamy beauty of the East, has forgotten both its father and its mother, and stands alone triumphant, the loveliest, brightest, and gayest of all the creations of the human mind and hand.

It has a literature of its own too, somewhat akin to its art, yet inferior to it, and lacking its unity, since there is a double stream in it. On the one hand is the court poet, the gentleman, Chaucer, with his Italianizing metres, and his formal recognition of the classical stories; on which, indeed, he builds a superstructure of the quaintest and most unadulterated mediævalism, as gay and bright as the architecture which his eyes beheld and his pen pictured for us, so clear, defined, and elegant it is; a sunny world even amidst its violence and passing troubles, like those of a happy child, the worst of them an amusement rather than a grief to the onlookers; a world that scarcely needed hope in its eager life of adventure and love, amidst the sunlit blossoming meadows, and green woods, and white begilded manor-houses. A kindly and human muse is Chaucer's, nevertheless, interested in and amused by all life, but of her very nature devoid of strong aspirations for the future; and that all the more, since, though the strong devotion and fierce piety of the ruder Middle Ages had by this time waned, and the Church was more often lightly mocked at than either feared or loved, still the habit of looking on this life as part of another yet remained: the world is fair and full of adventure; kind men and true and noble are in it to make one happy; fools also to laugh at, and rascals to be resisted, yet not wholly condemned; and when this world is over we shall still go on living in another which is a part of this. Look at all the picture, note all and live in all, and be as merry as you may, never forgetting that you are alive and that it is good to live.

That is the spirit of Chaucer's poetry; but alongside of it existed yet the ballad poetry of the people, wholly untouched by courtly elegance and classical pedantry; rude in art but never coarse, true to the backbone; instinct with indignation against wrong, and thereby expressing the hope that was in it; a protest of the poor against the rich, especially in those songs of the Foresters, which have been called the mediæval epic of revolt; no more gloomy than the gentleman's poetry, yet cheerful from courage, and not content. Half a dozen stanzas of it are worth a cartload of the whining introspective lyrics of to-day; and he who, when he has mastered the slight differences of language from our own daily speech, is not moved by it, does not understand what true poetry means nor what its aim is.

There is a third element in the literature of this time which you may call Lollard poetry, the great example of which is William Langland's "Piers Plowman." It is no bad corrective to Chaucer, and in form at least belongs wholly to the popular side; but it seems to me to show symptoms of the spirit of the rising middle class, and casts before it the shadow of the new master that was coming forward for the workman's oppression. But I must leave what more I have to say on this subject of the art and literature of the fourteenth century for another occasion. In what I have just said, I only wanted to point out to you that the Middle Ages had by this time come to the fullest growth; and that they could express in a form which was all their own, the ideas and life of the time.

That time was in a sense brilliant and progressive, and the life of the worker in it was better than it ever had been, and might compare with advantage with what it became in after periods and with what it is now; and indeed, looking back upon it, there are some minds and some moods that cannot help regretting it, and are not particularly scared by the idea of its violence and its lack of accurate knowledge of scientific detail.

However, one thing is clear to us now, the kind of thing which never is clear to most people living in such periods—namely, that whatever it was, it could not last, but must change into something else.

The complete feudalism of the fourteenth century fell, as systems always fall, by its own corruption, and by development of the innate seeds of change, some of which indeed had lain asleep during centuries, to wake up into activity long after the events which had created them were forgotten.

The feudal system was naturally one of open war; and the alliances, marriages, and other dealings, family with family, made by the king and potentates, were always leading them into war by giving them legal claims, or at least claims that could be legally pleaded, to the domains of other lords, who took advantage of their being on the spot, of their strength in men or money, or their popularity with the Baronage, to give immediate effect to their claims. Such a war was that by which Edward I. drew on England the enmity of the Scotch; and such again was the great war which Edward III. entered into with France. You must not suppose that there was anything in this war of a national, far less of a race, character. The last series of wars before this time I am now speaking of, in which race feelings counted for much, was the Crusades. This French war, I say, was neither national, racial, or tribal; it was the private business of a lord of the manor, claiming what he considered his legal rights of another lord, who had, as he thought, usurped them; and this claim his loyal feudatories were bound to take up for him; loyalty to a feudal superior, not patriotism to a country, was the virtue which Edward III.'s soldiers had to offer, if they had any call to be virtuous in that respect.

This war once started was hard to drop, partly because of the success that Edward had in it, falling as he did on France with the force of a country so much more homogeneous than it; and no doubt it was a war very disastrous to both countries, and so may be reckoned as amongst the causes which broke up the feudal system.

But the real causes of that break-up lay much deeper than that. The system was not capable of expansion in production; it was, in fact, as long as its integrity remained untouched, an army fed by slaves, who could not be properly and closely exploited; its free men proper might do something else in their leisure, and so produce art and literature, but their true business as members of a conquering tribe, their concerted business, was to fight. There was, indeed, a fringe of people between the serf and the free noble who produced the matters of handicraft which were needed for the latter, but deliberately, and, as we should now think, wastefully; and as these craftsmen and traders began to grow into importance and to push themselves, as they could not help doing, into the feudal hierarchy, as they acquired status, so the sickness of the feudal system increased on it, and the shadow of the coming commercialism fell upon it.

That any set of people who could claim to be other than the property of free men should not have definite rights differentiated sharply from those of other groups, was an idea that did not occur to the Middle Ages; therefore, as soon as men came into existence that were not serfs and were not nobles, they had to struggle for status by organizing themselves into associations that should come to be acknowledged members of the great feudal hierarchy; for indefinite and negative freedom was not allowed to any person in those days; if you had not status you did not exist except as an outlaw.

This is, briefly speaking, the motive power of necessity that lay behind the struggle of the town corporations and craft-gilds to be free, a struggle which, though it was to result in the breaking up of the mediæval hierarchy, began by an appearance of strengthening it by adding to its members, increasing its power of production, and so making it more stable for the time being.

About this struggle, and the kind of life which accompanied it, I may have to write another time, and so will not say more about it here. Except this, that it was much furthered by the change that gradually took place between the landlords and the class on whom all society rested, the serfs. These at first were men who had no more rights than chattel slaves had, except that mostly, as part of the stock of the manor, they could not be sold off it; they had to do all the work of the manor, and to earn their own livelihood off it as they best could. But as the power of production increased, owing to better methods of working, and as the country got to be more settled, their task-work became easier of performance and their own land more productive to them; and that tendency to the definition and differentiation of rights, moreover, was at work for their benefit, and the custom of the manor defined what their services were, and they began to acquire rights. From that time they ceased to be pure serfs, and began to tend towards becoming tenants, at first paying purely and simply service for their holdings, but gradually commuting that service for fines and money payment—for rent, in short.

Towards the close of the fourteenth century, after the country had been depopulated by the Black Death, and impoverished by the long war, the feudal lords of these copyholders and tenants began to regret the slackness with which their predecessors had exploited their property, the serfs, and to consider that under the new commercial light which had begun to dawn upon them they could do it much better if they only had their property a little more in hand; but it was too late, for their property had acquired rights, and therewithal had got strange visions into their heads of a time much better than that in which they lived, when even those rights should be supplanted by a condition of things in which the assertion of rights for any one set of men should no longer be needed, since all men should be free to enjoy the fruits of their own labour.

Of that came the great episode of the Peasants' War, led by men like Wat Tyler, Jack Straw, and John Ball, who indeed, with those they led, suffered for daring to be before their time, for the revolt was put down with cruelty worthy of an Irish landlord or a sweating capitalist of the present day; but, nevertheless, serfdom came to an end in England, if not because of the revolt, yet because of the events that made it, and thereby a death-wound was inflicted on the feudal system.

From that time onward the country, passing through the various troubles of a new French war of Henry V.'s time, and the War of the Roses, did not heed these faction fights much.

The workmen grew in prosperity, but also they began to rise into a new class, and a class beneath them of mere labourers who were not serfs began to form, and to lay the foundations of capitalistic production.

England got carried into the rising current of commercialism, and the rich men and landlords to turn their attention to the production of profit instead of the production of livelihood; the gild-less journeyman and the landless labourer slowly came into existence; the landlord got rid of his tenants all he could, turned tillage into pasture, and sweated the pastures to death in his eagerness for wool, which for him meant money and the breeding of money; till at last the place of the serf, which had stood empty, as it were, during a certain transition period, during which the non-capitalistic production was expanding up to its utmost limit, was filled by the proletarian working for the service of a master in a new fashion, a fashion which exploited and (woe worth the while!) exploits him very much more completely than the customs of the manor of the feudal period.

The life of the worker and the production of goods in this transition period, when Feudal society was sickening for its end, is a difficult and wide subject that requires separate treatment; at present I will leave the mediæval workman at the full development of that period which found him a serf bound to the manor, and which left him generally a yeoman or an artisan sharing the collective status of his gild.

The workman of to-day, if he could realize the position of his forerunner, has some reason to envy him: the feudal serf worked hard, and lived poorly, and produced a rough livelihood for his master; whereas the modern workman, working harder still, and living little if any better than the serf, produces for his master a state of luxury of which the old lord of the manor never dreamed. The workman's powers of production are multiplied a thousandfold; his own livelihood remains pretty much where it was. The balance goes to his master and the crowd of useless, draggled-tailed knaves and fools who pander to his idiotic sham desires, and who, under the pretentious title of the intellectual part of the middle classes, have in their turn taken the place of the mediæval jester.

Truly, if the Positivist motto, "Live for others," be taken in stark literality, the modern workman should be a good and wise man, since he has no chance of living for himself!

And yet, I wish he were wiser still; wise enough to make an end of the preaching of "Live on others," which is the motto set forth by commercialism to her favoured children.

Yet in one thing the modern proletarian has an advantage over the mediæval serf, and that advantage is a world in itself. Many a century lay between the serf and successful revolt, and though he tried it many a time and never lost heart, yet the coming change which his martyrdom helped on was not to be for him yet, but for the new masters of his successors. With us it is different. A few years of wearisome struggle against apathy and ignorance; a year or two of growing hope—and then who knows? Perhaps a few months, or perhaps a few days of the open struggle against brute force, with the mask off its face, and the sword in its hand, and then we are over the bar.

Who knows, I say? Yet this we know, that ahead of us, with nothing betwixt us except such incidents as are necessary to its development, lies the inevitable social revolution, which will bring about the end of mastery and the triumph of fellowship.

THE HOPES OF CIVILIZATION.

Every age has had its hopes, hopes that look to something beyond the life of the age itself, hopes that try to pierce into the future; and, strange to say, I believe that those hopes have been stronger not in the heyday of the epoch which has given them birth, but rather in its decadence and times of corruption: in sober truth it may well be that these hopes are but a reflection in those that live happily and comfortably of the vain longings of those others who suffer with little power of expressing their sufferings in an audible voice: when all goes well the happy world forgets these people and their desires, sure as it is that their woes are not dangerous to them the wealthy: whereas when the woes and grief of the poor begin to rise to a point beyond the endurance of men, fear conscious or unconscious falls upon the rich, and they begin to look about them to see what there may be among the elements of their society which may be used as palliatives for the misery which, long existing and ever growing greater among the slaves of that society, is now at last forcing itself on the attention of the masters. Times of change, disruption, and revolution are naturally times of hope also, and not seldom the hopes of something better to come are the first tokens that tell people that revolution is at hand, though commonly such tokens are no more believed than Cassandra's prophecies, or are even taken in a contrary sense by those who have anything to lose; since they look upon them as signs of the prosperity of the times, and the long endurance of that state of things which is so kind to them. Let us then see what the hopes of civilization are like to-day: for indeed I purpose speaking of our own times chiefly, and will leave for the present all mention of that older civilization which was destroyed by the healthy barbarism out of which our present society has grown.

Yet a few words may be necessary concerning the birth of our present epoch and the hopes it gave rise to, and what has become of them: that will not take us very far back in history; as to my mind our modern civilization begins with the stirring period about the time of the Reformation in England, the time which in the then more important countries of the Continent is known as the period of the Renaissance, the so-called new-birth of art and learning.

And first remember that this period includes the death-throes of feudalism, with all the good and evil which that system bore with it. For centuries past its end was getting ready by the gradual weakening of the bonds of the great hierarchy which held men together: the characteristics of those bonds were, theoretically at least, personal rights and personal duties between superior and inferior all down the scale; each man was born, so to say, subject to these conditions, and the mere accidents of his life could not free him from them: commerce, in our sense of the word, there was none; capitalistic manufacture, capitalistic exchange was unknown: to buy goods cheap that you might sell them dear was a legal offence (forestalling): to buy goods in the market in the morning and to sell them in the afternoon in the same place was not thought a useful occupation and was forbidden under the name of regrating; usury, instead of leading as now directly to the highest offices of the State, was thought wrong, and the profit of it mostly fell to the chosen people of God: the robbery of the workers, thought necessary then as now to the very existence of the State, was carried out quite crudely without any concealment or excuse by arbitrary taxation or open violence: on the other hand, life was easy, and common necessaries plenteous; the holidays of the Church were holidays in the modern sense of the word, downright play-days, and there were ninety-six obligatory ones: nor were the people tame and sheep-like, but as rough-handed and bold a set of good fellows as ever rubbed through life under the sun.

I remember three passages, from contemporary history or gossip, about the life of those times which luck has left us, and which illustrate curiously the change that has taken place in the habits of Englishmen. A lady writing from Norfolk 400 years ago to her husband in London, amidst various commissions for tapestries, groceries, and gowns, bids him also not to forget to bring back with him a good supply of cross-bows and bolts, since the windows of their hall were too low to be handy for long-bow shooting. A German traveller, writing quite at the end of the mediæval period, speaks of the English as the laziest and proudest people and the best cooks in Europe. A Spanish ambassador about the same period says, "These English live in houses built of sticks and mud, [87] but therein they fare as plenteously as lords."

Indeed, I confess that it is with a strange emotion that I recall these times and try to realize the life of our forefathers, men who were named like ourselves, spoke nearly the same tongue, lived on the same spots of earth, and therewithal were as different from us in manners, habits, ways of life and thought, as though they lived in another planet. The very face of the country has changed; not merely I mean in London and the great manufacturing centres, but through the country generally; there is no piece of English ground, except such places as Salisbury Plain, but bears witness to the amazing change which 400 years has brought upon us.

Not seldom I please myself with trying to realize the face of mediæval England; the many chases and great woods, the stretches of common tillage and common pasture quite unenclosed; the rough husbandry of the tilled parts, the unimproved breeds of cattle, sheep, and swine; especially the latter, so lank and long and lathy, looking so strange to us; the strings of packhorses along the bridle-roads, the scantiness of the wheel-roads, scarce any except those left by the Romans, and those made from monastery to monastery: the scarcity of bridges, and people using ferries instead, or fords where they could; the little towns, well bechurched, often walled; the villages just where they are now (except for those that have nothing but the church left to tell of them), but better and more populous; their churches, some big and handsome, some small and curious, but all crowded with altars and furniture, and gay with pictures and ornament; the many religious houses, with their glorious architecture; the beautiful manor-houses, some of them castles once, and survivals from an earlier period; some new and elegant; some out of all proportion small for the importance of their lords. How strange it would be to us if we could be landed in fourteenth century England; unless we saw the crest of some familiar hill, like that which yet bears upon it a symbol of an English tribe, and from which, looking down on the plain where Alfred was born, I once had many such ponderings, we should not know into what country of the world we were come: the name is left, scarce a thing else.

And when I think of this it quickens my hope of what may be: even so it will be with us in time to come; all will have changed, and another people will be dwelling here in England, who, although they may be of our blood and bear our name, will wonder how we lived in the nineteenth century.

Well, under all that rigidly ordered caste society of the fourteenth century, with its rough plenty, its sauntering life, its cool acceptance of rudeness and violence, there was going on a keen struggle of classes which carried with it the hope of progress of those days: the serfs gradually getting freed, and becoming some of them the town population, the first journeymen, or "free-labourers," so called, some of them the copyholders of agricultural land: the corporations of the towns gathered power, the craft-gilds grew into perfection and corruption, the power of the Crown increased, attended with nascent bureaucracy; in short, the middle class was forming underneath the outward show of feudalism still intact: and all was getting ready for the beginning of the great commercial epoch in whose latter days I would fain hope we are living. That epoch began with the portentous change of agriculture which meant cultivating for profit instead of for livelihood, and which carried with it the expropriation of the people from the land, the extinction of the yeoman, and the rise of the capitalist farmer; and the growth of the town population, which, swelled by the drift of the landless vagabonds and masterless men, grew into a definite proletariat or class of free-workmen; and their existence made that of the embryo capitalist-manufacturer also possible; and the reign of commercial contract and cash payment began to take the place of the old feudal hierarchy, with its many-linked chain of personal responsibilities. The latter half of the seventeenth century, the reign of Charles II., saw the last blow struck at this feudal system, when the landowners' military service was abolished, and they became simple owners of property that had no duties attached to it save the payment of a land-tax.

The hopes of the early part of the commercial period may be read in almost every book of the time, expressed in various degrees of dull or amusing pedantry, and show a naïf arrogance and contempt of the times just past through which nothing but the utmost simplicity of ignorance could have attained to. But the times were stirring, and gave birth to the most powerful individualities in many branches of literature, and More and Campanella, at least from the midst of the exuberant triumph of young commercialism, gave to the world prophetic hopes of times yet to come when that commercialism itself should have given place to the society which we hope will be the next transform of civilization into something else; into a new social life.

This period of early and exuberant hopes passed into the next stage of sober realization of many of them, for commerce grew and grew, and moulded all society to its needs: the workman of the sixteenth century worked still as an individual with little co-operation, and scarce any division of labour: by the end of the seventeenth he had become only a part of a group which by that time was in the handicrafts the real unit of production; division of labour even at that period had quite destroyed his individuality, and the worker was but part of a machine: all through the eighteenth century this system went on progressing towards perfection, till to most men of that period, to most of those who were in any way capable of expressing their thoughts, civilization had already reached a high stage of perfection, and was certain to go on from better to better.

These hopes were not on the surface of a very revolutionary kind, but nevertheless the class struggle still went on, and quite openly too; for the remains of feudality, aided by the mere mask and grimace of the religion, which was once a real part of the feudal system, hampered the progress of commerce sorely, and seemed a thousandfold more powerful than it really was; because in spite of the class struggle there was really a covert alliance between the powerful middle classes who were the children of commerce and their old masters the aristocracy; an unconscious understanding between them rather, in the midst of their contest, that certain matters were to be respected even by the advanced party: the contest and civil war between the king and the commons in England in the seventeenth century illustrates this well: the caution with which privilege was attacked in the beginning of the struggle, the unwillingness of all the leaders save a few enthusiasts to carry matters to their logical consequences, even when the march of events had developed the antagonism between aristocratic privilege and middle-class freedom of contract (so called); finally, the crystallization of the new order conquered by the sword of Naseby into a mongrel condition of things between privilege and bourgeois freedom, the defeat and grief of the purist Republicans, and the horror at and swift extinction of the Levellers, the pioneers of Socialism in that day, all point to the fact that the "party of progress," as we should call it now, was determined after all that privilege should not be abolished further than its own standpoint.

The seventeenth century ended in the great Whig revolution in England, and, as I said, commerce throve and grew enormously, and the power of the middle classes increased proportionately and all things seemed going smoothly with them, till at last in France the culminating corruption of a society, still nominally existing for the benefit of the privileged aristocracy, forced their hand: the old order of things, backed as it was by the power of the executive, by that semblance of overwhelming physical force which is the real and only cement of a society founded on the slavery of the many—the aristocratic power, seemed strong and almost inexpugnable: and since any stick will do to beat a dog with, the middle classes in France were forced to take up the first stick that lay ready to hand if they were not to give way to the aristocrats, which indeed the whole evolution of history forbade them to do. Therefore, as in England in the seventeenth century, the middle classes allied themselves to religious and republican, and even communistic enthusiasts, with the intention, firm though unexpressed, to keep them down when they had mounted to power by their means, so in France they had to ally themselves with the proletariat; which, shamefully oppressed and degraded as it had been, now for the first time in history began to feel its power, the power of numbers: by means of this help they triumphed over aristocratic privilege, but, on the other hand, although the proletariat was speedily reduced again to a position not much better than that it had held before the revolution, the part it played therein gave a new and terrible character to that revolution, and from that time forward the class struggle entered on to a new phase; the middle classes had gained a complete victory, which in France carried with it all the outward signs of victory, though in England they chose to consider a certain part of themselves an aristocracy, who had indeed little signs of aristocracy about them either for good or for evil, being in very few cases of long descent, and being in their manners and ideas unmistakably bourgeois.

So was accomplished the second act of the great class struggle with whose first act began the age of commerce; as to the hopes of this period of the revolution we all know how extravagant they were; what a complete regeneration of the world was expected to result from the abolition of the grossest form of privilege; and I must say that, before we mock at the extravagance of those hopes, we should try to put ourselves in the place of those that held them, and try to conceive how the privilege of the old noblesse must have galled the respectable well-to-do people of that time. Well, the reasonable part of those hopes were realized by the revolution; in other words, it accomplished what it really aimed at, the freeing of commerce from the fetters of sham feudality; or, in other words, the destruction of aristocratic privilege. The more extravagant part of the hopes expressed by the eighteenth century revolution were vague enough, and tended in the direction of supposing that the working classes would be benefited by what was to the interest of the middle class in some way quite unexplained—by a kind of magic, one may say—which welfare of the workers, as it was never directly aimed at, but only hoped for by the way, so also did not come about by any such magical means, and the triumphant middle classes began gradually to find themselves looked upon no longer as rebellious servants, but as oppressive masters.

The middle class had freed commerce from her fetters of privilege, and had freed thought from her fetters of theology, at least partially; but it had not freed, nor attempted to free, labour from its fetters. The leaders of the French Revolution, even amidst the fears, suspicions and slaughter of the Terror, upheld the rights of "property" so called, though a new pioneer or prophet appeared in France, analogous in some respects to the Levellers of Cromwell's time, but, as might be expected, far more advanced and reasonable than they were. Gracchus Babeuf and his fellows were treated as criminals, and died or suffered the torture of prison for attempting to put into practice those words which the Republic still carried on its banners, and Liberty, Fraternity, and Equality were interpreted in a middle-class, or if you please a Jesuitical, sense, as the rewards of success for those who could struggle into an exclusive class; and at last property had to be defended by a military adventurer, and the Revolution seemed to have ended with Napoleonism.

Nevertheless, the Revolution was not dead, nor was it possible to say thus far and no further to the rising tide. Commerce, which had created the propertyless proletariat throughout civilization had still another part to play, which is not yet played out; she had and has to teach the workers to know what they are; to educate them, to consolidate them, and not only to give them aspirations for their advancement as a class, but to make means for them to realize those aspirations. All this she did, nor loitered in her work either; from the beginning of the nineteenth century the history of civilization is really the history of the last of the class-struggles which was inaugurated by the French Revolution; and England, who all through the times of the Revolution and the Cæsarism which followed it appeared to be the steady foe of Revolution, was really as steadily furthering it; her natural conditions, her store of coal and minerals, her temperate climate, extensive sea-board and many harbours, and lastly her position as the outpost of Europe looking into America across the ocean, doomed her to be for a time at least the mistress of the commerce of the civilized world, and its agent with barbarous and semi-barbarous countries. The necessities of this destiny drove her into the implacable war with France, a war which, nominally waged on behalf of monarchical principles, was really, though doubtless unconsciously, carried on for the possession of the foreign and colonial markets. She came out victorious from that war, and fully prepared to take advantage of the industrial revolution which had been going on the while, and which I now ask you to note.

I have said that the eighteenth century perfected the system of labour which took the place of the mediæval system, under which a workman individually carried his piece of work all through its various stages from the first to the last.

This new system, the first change in industrial production since the Middle Ages, is known as the system of division of labour, wherein, as I said, the unit of labour is a group, not a man; the individual workman in this system is kept life-long at the performance of some task quite petty in itself, and which he soon masters, and having mastered it has nothing more to do but to go on increasing his speed of hand under the spur of competition with his fellows, until he has become the perfect machine which it is his ultimate duty to become, since without attaining to that end he must die or become a pauper. You can well imagine how this glorious invention of division of labour, this complete destruction of individuality in the workman, and his apparent hopeless enslavement to his profit-grinding master, stimulated the hopes of civilization; probably more hymns have been sung in praise of division of labour, more sermons preached about it, than have done homage to the precept, "do unto others as ye would they should do unto you."

To drop all irony, surely this was one of those stages of civilization at which one might well say that, if it was to stop there, it was a pity that it had ever got so far. I have had to study books and methods of work of the eighteenth century a good deal, French chiefly; and I must say that the impression made on me by that study is that the eighteenth century artisan must have been a terrible product of civilization, and quite in a condition to give rise to hopes—of the torch, the pike, and the guillotine.

However, civilization was not going to stop there; having turned the man into a machine, the next stage for commerce to aim at was to contrive machines which would widely dispense with human labour; nor was this aim altogether disappointed.

Now, at first sight it would seem that having got the workman into such a plight as he was, as the slave of division of labour, this new invention of machines which should free him from a part of his labour at least, could be nothing to him but an unmixed blessing. Doubtless it will prove to have been so in the end, when certain institutions have been swept away which most people now look on as eternal; but a longish time has passed during which the workman's hopes of civilization have been disappointed, for those who invented the machines, or rather who profited by their invention, did not aim at the saving of labour in the sense of reducing the labour which each man had to do, but, first taking it for granted that every workman would have to work as long as he could stand up to it, aimed, under those conditions of labour, at producing the utmost possible amount of goods which they could sell at a profit.

Need I dwell on the fact that, under these circumstances, the invention of the machines has benefited the workman but little even to this day?

Nay, at first they made his position worse than it had been: for, being thrust on the world very suddenly, they distinctly brought about an industrial revolution, changing everything suddenly and completely; industrial productiveness was increased prodigiously, but so far from the workers reaping the benefit of this, they were thrown out of work in enormous numbers, while those who were still employed were reduced from the position of skilled artisans to that of unskilled labourers: the aims of their masters being, as I said, to make a profit, they did not trouble themselves about this as a class, but took it for granted that it was something that couldn't be helped and didn't hurt them; nor did they think of offering to the workers that compensation for harassed interests which they have since made a point of claiming so loudly for themselves.

This was the state of things which followed on the conclusion of European peace, and even that peace itself rather made matters worse than better, by the sudden cessation of all war industries, and the throwing on to the market many thousands of soldiers and sailors: in short, at no period of English history was the condition of the workers worse than in the early years of the nineteenth century.

There seem during this period to have been two currents of hope that had reference to the working classes: the first affected the masters, the second the men.

In England, and, in what I am saying of this period, I am chiefly thinking of England, the hopes of the richer classes ran high; and no wonder; for England had by this time become the mistress of the markets of the world, and also, as the people of that period were never weary of boasting, the workshop of the world: the increase in the riches of the country was enormous, even at the early period I am thinking of now—prior to '48, I mean—though it increased much more speedily in times that we have all seen: but part of the jubilant hopes of this newly rich man concerned his servants, the instruments of his fortune: it was hoped that the population in general would grow wiser, better educated, thriftier, more industrious, more comfortable; for which hope there was surely some foundation, since man's mastery over the forces of Nature was growing yearly towards completion; but you see these benevolent gentlemen supposed that these hopes would be realized perhaps by some unexplained magic as aforesaid, or perhaps by the working-classes, at their own expense, by the exercise of virtues supposed to be specially suited to their condition, and called, by their masters, "thrift" and "industry." For this latter supposition there was no foundation: indeed, the poor wretches who were thrown out of work by the triumphant march of commerce had perforce worn thrift threadbare, and could hardly better their exploits in that direction; while as to those who worked in the factories, or who formed the fringe of labour elsewhere, industry was no new gospel to them, since they already worked as long as they could work without dying at the loom, the spindle, or the stithy. They for their part had their hopes, vague enough as to their ultimate aim, but expressed in the passing day by a very obvious tendency to revolt: this tendency took various forms, which I cannot dwell on here, but settled down at last into Chartism: about which I must speak a few words: but first I must mention, I can scarce do more, the honoured name of Robert Owen, as representative of the nobler hopes of his day, just as More was of his, and the lifter of the torch of Socialism amidst the dark days of the confusion consequent on the reckless greed of the early period of the great factory industries.

That the conditions under which man lived could affect his life and his deeds infinitely, that not selfish greed and ceaseless contention, but brotherhood and co-operation were the bases of true society, was the gospel which he preached and also practised with a single-heartedness, devotion, and fervour of hope which have never been surpassed: he was the embodied hope of the days when the advance of knowledge and the sufferings of the people thrust revolutionary hope upon those thinkers who were not in some form or other in the pay of the sordid masters of society.

As to the Chartist agitation, there is this to be said of it, that it was thoroughly a working-class movement, and it was caused by the simplest and most powerful of all causes—hunger. It is noteworthy that it was strongest, especially in its earlier days, in the Northern and Midland manufacturing districts—that is, in the places which felt the distress caused by the industrial revolution most sorely and directly; it sprang up with particular vigour in the years immediately following the great Reform Bill; and it has been remarked that disappointment of the hopes which that measure had cherished had something to do with its bitterness. As it went on, obvious causes for failure were developed in it; self-seeking leadership; futile discussion of the means of making the change, before organization of the party was perfected; blind fear of ultimate consequences on the part of some, blind disregard to immediate consequences on the part of others; these were the surface reasons for its failure: but it would have triumphed over all these and accomplished revolution in England, if it had not been for causes deeper and more vital than these. Chartism differed from mere Radicalism in being a class movement; but its aim was after all political rather than social. The Socialism of Robert Owen fell short of its object because it did not understand that, as long as there is a privileged class in possession of the executive power, they will take good care that their economical position, which enables them to live on the unpaid labour of the people, is not tampered with: the hopes of the Chartists were disappointed because they did not understand that true political freedom is impossible to people who are economically enslaved: there is no first and second in these matters, the two must go hand in hand together: we cannot live as we will, and as we should, as long as we allow people to govern us whose interest it is that we should live as they will, and by no means as we should; neither is it any use claiming the right to manage our own business unless we are prepared to have some business of our own: these two aims united mean the furthering of the class struggle till all classes are abolished—the divorce of one from the other is fatal to any hope of social advancement.

Chartism therefore, though a genuine popular movement, was incomplete in its aims and knowledge; the time was not yet come and it could not triumph openly; but it would be a mistake to say that it failed utterly: at least it kept alive the holy flame of discontent; it made it possible for us to attain to the political goal of democracy, and thereby to advance the cause of the people by the gain of a stage from whence could be seen the fresh gain to be aimed at.

I have said that the time for revolution had not then come: the great wave of commercial success went on swelling, and though the capitalists would if they had dared have engrossed the whole of the advantages thereby gained at the expense of their wage slaves, the Chartist revolt warned them that it was not safe to attempt it. They were forced to try to allay discontent by palliative measures. They had to allow Factory Acts to be passed regulating the hours and conditions of labour of women and children, and consequently of men also in some of the more important and consolidated industries; they were forced to repeal the ferocious laws against combination among the workmen; so that the Trades Unions won for themselves a legal position and became a power in the labour question, and were able by means of strikes and threats of strikes to regulate the wages granted to the workers, and to raise the standard of livelihood for a certain part of the skilled workmen and the labourers associated with them: though the main part of the unskilled, including the agricultural workmen, were no better off than before.

Thus was damped down the flame of a discontent vague in its aims, and passionately crying out for what, if granted, it could not have used: twenty years ago any one hinting at the possibility of serious class discontent in this country would have been looked upon as a madman; in fact, the well-to-do and cultivated were quite unconscious (as many still are) that there was any class distinction in this country other than what was made by the rags and cast clothes of feudalism, which in a perfunctory manner they still attacked.

There was no sign of revolutionary feeling in England twenty years ago: the middle class were so rich that they had no need to hope for anything—but a heaven which they did not believe in: the well-to-do working men did not hope, since they were not pinched and had no means of learning their degraded position: and lastly, the drudges of the proletariat had such hope as charity, the hospital, the workhouse, and kind death at last could offer them.

In this stock-jobbers' heaven let us leave our dear countrymen for a little, while I say a few words about the affairs of the people on the continent of Europe. Things were not quite so smooth for the fleecer there: Socialist thinkers and writers had arisen about the same time as Robert Owen; St. Simon, Proudhon, Fourier and his followers kept up the traditions of hope in the midst of a bourgeois world. Amongst these Fourier is the one that calls for most attention: since his doctrine of the necessity and possibility of making labour attractive is one which Socialism can by no means do without. France also kept up the revolutionary and insurrectionary tradition, the result of something like hope still fermenting amongst the proletariat: she fell at last into the clutches of a second Cæsarism developed by the basest set of sharpers, swindlers, and harlots that ever insulted a country, and of whom our own happy bourgeois at home made heroes and heroines: the hideous open corruption of Parisian society, to which, I repeat, our respectable classes accorded heartfelt sympathy, was finally swept away by the horrors of a race war: the defeats and disgraces of this war developed, on the one hand, an increase in the wooden implacability and baseness of the French bourgeois, but on the other made way for revolutionary hope to spring again, from which resulted the attempt to establish society on the basis of the freedom of labour, which we call the Commune of Paris of 1871. Whatever mistakes or imprudences were made in this attempt, and all wars blossom thick with such mistakes, I will leave the reactionary enemies of the people's cause to put forward: the immediate and obvious result was the slaughter of thousands of brave and honest revolutionists at the hands of the respectable classes, the loss in fact of an army for the popular cause: but we may be sure that the results of the Commune will not stop there: to all Socialists that heroic attempt will give hope and ardour in the cause as long as it is to be won; we feel as though the Paris workman had striven to bring the day-dawn for us, and had lifted us the sun's rim over the horizon, never to set in utter darkness again: of such attempts one must say, that though those who perished in them might have been put in a better place in the battle, yet after all brave men never die for nothing, when they die for principle.

Let us shift from France to Germany before we get back to England again, and conclude with a few words about our hopes at the present day. To Germany we owe the school of economists, at whose head stands the name of Karl Marx, who have made modern Socialism what it is: the earlier Socialist writers and preachers based their hopes on man being taught to see the desirableness of co-operation taking the place of competition, and adopting the change voluntarily and consciously, and they trusted to schemes more or less artificial being tried and accepted, although such schemes were necessarily constructed out of the materials which capitalistic society offered: but the new school, starting with an historical view of what had been, and seeing that a law of evolution swayed all events in it, was able to point out to us that the evolution was still going on, and that, whether Socialism be desirable or not, it is at least inevitable. Here then was at last a hope of a different kind to any that had gone before it; and the German and Austrian workmen were not slow to learn the lesson founded on this theory; from being one of the most backward countries in Europe in the movement, before Lassalle started his German workman's party in 1863, Germany soon became the leader in it: Bismarck's repressive law has only acted on opinion there, as the roller does to the growing grass—made it firmer and stronger; and whatever vicissitudes may be the fate of the party as a party, there can be no doubt that Socialistic opinion is firmly established there, and that when the time is ripe for it that opinion will express itself in action.

Now, in all I have been saying, I have been wanting you to trace the fact that, ever since the establishment of commercialism on the ruins of feudality, there has been growing a steady feeling on the part of the workers that they are a class dealt with as a class, and in like manner to deal with others; and that as this class feeling has grown, so also has grown with it a consciousness of the antagonism between their class and the class which employs it, as the phrase goes; that is to say, which lives by means of its labour.

Now it is just this growing consciousness of the fact that as long as there exists in society a propertied class living on the labour of a propertyless one, there must be a struggle always going on between those two classes—it is just the dawning knowledge of this fact which should show us what civilization can hope for—namely, transformation into true society, in which there will no longer be classes with their necessary struggle for existence and superiority: for the antagonism of classes which began in all simplicity between the master and the chattel slave of ancient society, and was continued between the feudal lord and the serf of mediæval society, has gradually become the contention between the capitalist developed from the workman of the last-named period, and the wage-earner: in the former struggle the rise of the artisan and villenage tenant created a new class, the middle class, while the place of the old serf was filled by the propertyless labourer, with whom the middle class, which has absorbed the aristocracy, is now face to face: the struggle between the classes therefore is once again a simple one, as in the days of the classical peoples; but since there is no longer any strong race left out of civilization, as in the time of the disruption of Rome, the whole struggle in all its simplicity between those who have and those who lack is within civilization.

Moreover, the capitalist or modern slave-owner has been forced by his very success, as we have seen, to organize his slaves, the wage-earners, into a co-operation for production so well arranged that it requires little but his own elimination to make it a foundation for communal life: in the teeth also of the experience of past ages, he has been compelled to allow a modicum of education to the propertyless, and has not even been able to deprive them wholly of political rights; his own advance in wealth and power has bred for him the very enemy who is doomed to make an end of him.

But will there be any new class to take the place of the present proletariat when that has triumphed, as it must do, over the present privileged class? We cannot foresee the future, but we may fairly hope not: at least we cannot see any signs of such a new class forming. It is impossible to see how destruction of privilege can stop short of absolute equality of condition; pure Communism is the logical deduction from the imperfect form of the new society, which is generally differentiated from it as Socialism.

Meantime, it is this simplicity and directness of the growing contest which above all things presents itself as a terror to the conservative instinct of the present day. Many among the middle class who are sincerely grieved and shocked at the condition of the proletariat which civilization has created, and even alarmed by the frightful inequalities which it fosters, do nevertheless shudder back from the idea of the class struggle, and strive to shut their eyes to the fact that it is going on. They try to think that peace is not only possible, but natural, between the two classes, the very essence of whose existence is that each can only thrive by what it manages to force the other to yield to it. They propose to themselves the impossible problem of raising the inferior or exploited classes into a position in which they will cease to struggle against the superior classes, while the latter will not cease to exploit them. This absurd position drives them into the concoction of schemes for bettering the condition of the working classes at their own expense, some of them futile, some merely fantastic; or they may be divided again into those which point out the advantages and pleasures of involuntary asceticism, and reactionary plans for importing the conditions of the production and life of the Middle Ages (wholly misunderstood by them, by the way) into the present system of the capitalist farmer, the great industries, and the universal world-market. Some see a solution of the social problem in sham co-operation, which is merely an improved form of joint-stockery: others preach thrift to (precarious) incomes of eighteen shillings a week, and industry to men killing themselves by inches in working overtime, or to men whom the labour-market has rejected as not wanted: others beg the proletarians not to breed so fast; an injunction the compliance with which might be at first of advantage to the proletarians themselves in their present condition, but would certainly undo the capitalists, if it were carried to any lengths, and would lead through ruin and misery to the violent outbreak of the very revolution which these timid people are so anxious to forego.

Then there are others who, looking back on the past, and perceiving that the workmen of the Middle Ages lived in more comfort and self-respect than ours do, even though they were subjected to the class rule of men who were looked on as another order of beings than they, think that if those conditions of life could be reproduced under our better political conditions the question would be solved for a time at least. Their schemes may be summed up in attempts, more or less preposterously futile, to graft a class of independent peasants on our system of wages and capital. They do not understand that this system of independent workmen, producing almost entirely for the consumption of themselves and their neighbours, and exploited by the upper classes by obvious taxes on their labour, which was not otherwise organized or interfered with by the exploiters, was what in past times took the place of our system, in which the workers sell their labour in the competitive market to masters who have in their hands the whole organization of the markets, and that these two systems are mutually destructive.

Others again believe in the possibility of starting from our present workhouse system, for the raising of the lowest part of the working population into a better condition, but do not trouble themselves as to the position of the workers who are fairly above the condition of pauperism, or consider what part they will play in the contest for a better livelihood. And, lastly, quite a large number of well-intentioned persons belonging to the richer classes believe, that in a society that compels competition for livelihood, and holds out to the workers as a stimulus to exertion the hope of their rising into a monopolist class of non-producers, it is yet possible to "moralize" capital (to use a slang phrase of the Positivists): that is to say, that a sentiment imported from a religion which looks upon another world as the true sphere of action for mankind, will override the necessities of our daily life in this world. This curious hope is founded on the feeling that a sentiment antagonistic to the full development of commercialism exists and is gaining ground, and that this sentiment is an independent growth of the ethics of the present epoch. As a matter of fact, admitting its existence, as I think we must do, it is the birth of the sense of insecurity which is the shadow cast before by the approaching dissolution of modern society founded on wage-slavery.

The greater part of these schemes aim, though seldom with the consciousness of their promoters, at the creation of a new middle-class out of the wage-earning class, and at their expense, just as the present middle-class was developed out of the serf-population of the early Middle Ages. It may be possible that such a further development of the middle-class lies before us, but it will not be brought about by any such artificial means as the abovementioned schemes. If it comes at all, it must be produced by events, which at present we cannot foresee, acting on our commercial system, and revivifying for a little time, maybe, that Capitalist Society which now seems sickening towards its end.

For what is visible before us in these days is the competitive commercial system killing itself by its own force: profits lessening, businesses growing bigger and bigger, the small employer of labour thrust out of his function, and the aggregation of capital increasing the numbers of the lower middle-class from above rather than from below, by driving the smaller manufacturer into the position of a mere servant to the bigger. The productivity of labour also increasing out of all proportion to the capacity of the capitalists to manage the market or deal with the labour supply: lack of employment therefore becoming chronic, and discontent therewithal.

All this on the one hand. On the other, the workmen claiming everywhere political equality, which cannot long be denied; and education spreading, so that what between the improvement in the education of the working-class and the continued amazing fatuity of that of the upper classes, there is a distinct tendency to equalization here; and, as I have hinted above, all history shows us what a danger to society may be a class at once educated and socially degraded: though, indeed, no history has yet shown us—what is swiftly advancing upon us—a class which, though it shall have attained knowledge, shall lack utterly the refinement and self-respect which come from the union of knowledge with leisure and ease of life. The growth of such a class may well make the "cultured" people of to-day tremble.

Whatever, therefore, of unforeseen and unconceived-of may lie in the womb of the future, there is nothing visible before us but a decaying system, with no outlook but ever-increasing entanglement and blindness, and a new system, Socialism, the hope of which is ever growing clearer in men's minds—a system which not only sees how labour can be freed from its present fetters, and organized unwastefully, so as to produce the greatest possible amount of wealth for the community and for every member of it, but which bears with it its own ethics and religion and æsthetics: that is the hope and promise of a new and higher life in all ways. So that even if those unforeseen economical events above spoken of were to happen, and put off for a while the end of our Capitalist system, the latter would drag itself along as an anomaly cursed by all, a mere clog on the aspirations of humanity.

It is not likely that it will come to that: in all probability the logical outcome of the latter days of Capitalism will go step by step with its actual history: while all men, even its declared enemies, will be working to bring Socialism about, the aims of those who have learned to believe in the certainty and beneficence of its advent will become clearer, their methods for realizing it clearer also, and at last ready to hand. Then will come that open acknowledgment for the necessity of the change (an acknowledgment coming from the intelligence of civilization) which is commonly called Revolution. It is no use prophesying as to the events which will accompany that revolution, but to a reasonable man it seems unlikely to the last degree, or we will say impossible, that a moral sentiment will induce the proprietary classes—those who live by owning the means of production which the unprivileged classes must needs use—to yield up this privilege uncompelled; all one can hope is that they will see the implicit threat of compulsion in the events of the day, and so yield with a good grace to the terrible necessity of forming part of a world in which all, including themselves, will work honestly and live easily.

THE AIMS OF ART.

In considering the Aims of Art, that is, why men toilsomely cherish and practise Art, I find myself compelled to generalize from the only specimen of humanity of which I know anything; to wit, myself. Now, when I think of what it is that I desire, I find that I can give it no other name than happiness. I want to be happy while I live; for as for death, I find that, never having experienced it, I have no conception of what it means, and so cannot even bring my mind to bear upon it. I know what it is to live; I cannot even guess what it is to be dead. Well, then, I want to be happy, and even sometimes, say generally, to be merry; and I find it difficult to believe that that is not the universal desire: so that, whatever tends towards that end I cherish with all my best endeavour. Now, when I consider my life further, I find out, or seem to, that it is under the influence of two dominating moods, which for lack of better words I must call the mood of energy and the mood of idleness: these two moods are now one, now the other, always crying out in me to be satisfied. When the mood of energy is upon me, I must be doing something, or I become mopish and unhappy; when the mood of idleness is on me, I find it hard indeed if I cannot rest and let my mind wander over the various pictures, pleasant or terrible, which my own experience or my communing with the thoughts of other men, dead or alive, have fashioned in it; and if circumstances will not allow me to cultivate this mood of idleness, I find I must at the best pass through a period of pain till I can manage to stimulate my mood of energy to take its place and make me happy again. And if I have no means wherewith to rouse up that mood of energy to do its duty in making me happy, and I have to toil while the idle mood is upon me, then am I unhappy indeed, and almost wish myself dead, though I do not know what that means.

Furthermore, I find that while in the mood of idleness memory amuses me, in the mood of energy hope cheers me; which hope is sometimes big and serious, and sometimes trivial, but that without it there is no happy energy. Again, I find that while I can sometimes satisfy this mood by merely exercising it in work that has no result beyond the passing hour—in play, in short—yet that it presently wearies of that and gets languid, the hope therein being too trivial, and sometimes even scarcely real; and that on the whole, to satisfy my master the mood, I must either be making something or making believe to make it.

Well, I believe that all men's lives are compounded of these two moods in various proportions, and that this explains why they have always, with more or less of toil, cherished and practised art.

Why should they have touched it else, and so added to the labour which they could not choose but do in order to live? It must have been done for their pleasure, since it has only been in very elaborate civilizations that a man could get other men to keep him alive merely to produce works of art, whereas all men that have left any signs of their existence behind them have practised art.

I suppose, indeed, that nobody will be inclined to deny that the end proposed by a work of art is always to please the person whose senses are to be made conscious of it. It was done for some one who was to be made happier by it; his idle or restful mood was to be amused by it, so that the vacancy which is the besetting evil of that mood might give place to pleased contemplation, dreaming, or what you will; and by this means he would not so soon be driven into his workful or energetic mood: he would have more enjoyment, and better.

The restraining of restlessness, therefore, is clearly one of the essential aims of art, and few things could add to the pleasure of life more than this. There are, to my knowledge, gifted people now alive who have no other vice than this of restlessness, and seemingly no other curse in their lives to make them unhappy: but that is enough; it is "the little rift within the lute." Restlessness makes them hapless men and bad citizens.

But granting, as I suppose you all will do, that this is a most important function for art to fulfil, the question next comes, at what price do we obtain it? I have admitted that the practice of art has added to the labour of mankind, though I believe in the long run it will not do so; but in adding to the labour of man has it added, so far, to his pain? There always have been people who would at once say yes to that question; so that there have been and are two sets of people who dislike and contemn art as an embarrassing folly. Besides the pious ascetics, who look upon it as a worldly entanglement which prevents men from keeping their minds fixed on the chances of their individual happiness or misery in the next world; who, in short, hate art, because they think that it adds to man's earthly happiness—besides these, there are also people who, looking on the struggle of life from the most reasonable point that they know of, contemn the arts because they think that they add to man's slavery by increasing the sum of his painful labour: if this were the case, it would still, to my mind, be a question whether it might not be worth the while to endure the extra pain of labour for the sake of the extra pleasure added to rest; assuming, for the present, equality of condition among men. But it seems to me that it is not the case that the practice of art adds to painful labour; nay more, I believe that, if it did, art would never have arisen at all, would certainly not be discernible, as it is, among peoples in whom only the germs of civilization exist. In other words, I believe that art cannot be the result of external compulsion; the labour which goes to produce it is voluntary, and partly undertaken for the sake of the labour itself, partly for the sake of the hope of producing something which, when done, shall give pleasure to the user of it. Or, again, this extra labour, when it is extra, is undertaken with the aim of satisfying that mood of energy by employing it to produce something worth doing, and which, therefore, will keep before the worker a lively hope while he is working; and also by giving it work to do in which there is absolute immediate pleasure. Perhaps it is difficult to explain to the non-artistic capacity that this definite sensuous pleasure is always present in the handiwork of the deft workman when he is working successfully, and that it increases in proportion to the freedom and individuality of the work. Also you must understand that this production of art, and consequent pleasure in work, is not confined to the production of matters which are works of art only, like pictures, statues, and so forth, but has been and should be a part of all labour in some form or other: so only will the claims of the mood of energy be satisfied.

Therefore the Aim of Art is to increase the happiness of men, by giving them beauty and interest of incident to amuse their leisure, and prevent them wearying even of rest, and by giving them hope and bodily pleasure in their work; or, shortly, to make man's work happy and his rest fruitful. Consequently, genuine art is an unmixed blessing to the race of man.

But as the word "genuine" is a large qualification, I must ask leave to attempt to draw some practical conclusions from this assertion of the Aims of Art, which will, I suppose, or indeed hope, lead us into some controversy on the subject; because it is futile indeed to expect any one to speak about art, except in the most superficial way, without encountering those social problems which all serious men are thinking of; since art is and must be, either in its abundance or its barrenness, in its sincerity or its hollowness, the expression of the society amongst which it exists.

First, then, it is clear to me that, at the present time, those who look widest at things and deepest into them are quite dissatisfied with the present state of the arts, as they are also with the present condition of society. This I say in the teeth of the supposed revivification of art which has taken place of late years: in fact, that very excitement about the arts amongst a part of the cultivated people of to-day does but show on how firm a basis the dissatisfaction above mentioned rests. Forty years ago there was much less talk about art, much less practice of it, than there is now; and that is specially true of the architectural arts, which I shall mostly have to speak about now. People have consciously striven to raise the dead in art since that time, and with some superficial success. Nevertheless, in spite of this conscious effort, I must tell you that England, to a person who can feel and understand beauty, was a less grievous place to live in then than it is now; and we who feel what art means know well, though we do not often dare to say so, that forty years hence it will be a more grievous place to us than it is now if we still follow up the road we are on. Less than forty years ago—about thirty—I first saw the city of Rouen, then still in its outward aspect a piece of the Middle Ages: no words can tell you how its mingled beauty, history, and romance took hold on me; I can only say that, looking back on my past life, I find it was the greatest pleasure I have ever had: and now it is a pleasure which no one can ever have again: it is lost to the world for ever. At that time I was an undergraduate of Oxford. Though not so astounding, so romantic, or at first sight so mediæval as the Norman city, Oxford in those days still kept a great deal of its earlier loveliness: and the memory of its grey streets as they then were has been an abiding influence and pleasure in my life, and would be greater still if I could only forget what they are now—a matter of far more importance than the so-called learning of the place could have been to me in any case, but which, as it was, no one tried to teach me, and I did not try to learn. Since then the guardians of this beauty and romance so fertile of education, though professedly engaged in "the higher education" (as the futile system of compromises which they follow is nick-named), have ignored it utterly, have made its preservation give way to the pressure of commercial exigencies, and are determined apparently to destroy it altogether. There is another pleasure for the world gone down the wind; here, again, the beauty and romance have been uselessly, causelessly, most foolishly thrown away.

These two cases are given simply because they have been fixed in my mind; they are but types of what is going on everywhere throughout civilization: the world is everywhere growing uglier and more commonplace, in spite of the conscious and very strenuous efforts of a small group of people towards the revival of art, which are so obviously out of joint with the tendency of the age that, while the uncultivated have not even heard of them, the mass of the cultivated look upon them as a joke, and even that they are now beginning to get tired of.

Now, if it be true, as I have asserted, that genuine art is an unmixed blessing to the world, this is a serious matter; for at first sight it seems to show that there will soon be no art at all in the world, which will thus lose an unmixed blessing; it can ill afford to do that, I think.

For art, if it has to die, has worn itself out, and its aim will be a thing forgotten; and its aim was to make work happy and rest fruitful. Is all work to be unhappy, all rest unfruitful, then? Indeed, if art is to perish, that will be the case, unless something is to take its place—something at present unnamed, undreamed of.

I do not think that anything will take the place of art; not that I doubt the ingenuity of man, which seems to be boundless in the direction of making himself unhappy, but because I believe the springs of art in the human mind to be deathless, and also because it seems to me easy to see the causes of the present obliteration of the arts.

For we civilized people have not given them up consciously, or of our free will; we have been forced to give them up. Perhaps I can illustrate that by the detail of the application of machinery to the production of things in which artistic form of some sort is possible. Why does a reasonable man use a machine? Surely to save his labour. There are some things which a machine can do as well as a man's hand, plus a tool, can do them. He need not, for instance, grind his corn in a hand-quern; a little trickle of water, a wheel, and a few simple contrivances will do it all perfectly well, and leave him free to smoke his pipe and think, or to carve the handle of his knife. That, so far, is unmixed gain in the use of a machine—always, mind you, supposing equality of condition among men; no art is lost, leisure or time for more pleasurable work is gained. Perhaps a perfectly reasonable and free man would stop there in his dealings with machinery; but such reason and freedom are too much to expect, so let us follow our machine-inventor a step farther. He has to weave plain cloth, and finds doing so dullish on the one hand, and on the other that a power-loom will weave the cloth nearly as well as a hand-loom: so, in order to gain more leisure or time for more pleasurable work, he uses a power-loom, and foregoes the small advantage of the little extra art in the cloth. But so doing, as far as the art is concerned, he has not got a pure gain; he has made a bargain between art and labour, and got a makeshift as a consequence. I do not say that he may not be right in so doing, but that he has lost as well as gained. Now, this is as far as a man who values art and is reasonable would go in the matter of machinery as long as he was free—that is, was not forced to work for another man's profit; so long as he was living in a society that had accepted equality of condition. Carry the machine used for art a step farther, and he becomes an unreasonable man, if he values art and is free. To avoid misunderstanding, I must say that I am thinking of the modern machine, which is as it were alive, and to which the man is auxiliary, and not of the old machine, the improved tool, which is auxiliary to the man, and only works as long as his hand is thinking; though I will remark, that even this elementary form of machine has to be dropped when we come to the higher and more intricate forms of art. Well, as to the machine proper used for art, when it gets to the stage above dealing with a necessary production that has accidentally some beauty about it, a reasonable man with a feeling for art will only use it when he is forced to. If he thinks he would like ornament, for instance, and knows that the machine cannot do it properly, and does not care to spend the time to do it properly, why should he do it at all? He will not diminish his leisure for the sake of making something he does not want unless some man or band of men force him to it; so he will either go without the ornament, or sacrifice some of his leisure to have it genuine. That will be a sign that he wants it very much, and that it will be worth his trouble: in which case, again, his labour on it will not be mere trouble, but will interest and please him by satisfying the needs of his mood of energy.

This, I say, is how a reasonable man would act if he were free from man's compulsion; not being free, he acts very differently. He has long passed the stage at which machines are only used for doing work repulsive to an average man, or for doing what could be as well done by a machine as a man, and he instinctively expects a machine to be invented whenever any product of industry becomes sought after. He is the slave to machinery; the new machine must be invented, and when invented he must—I will not say use it, but be used by it, whether he likes it or not.

But why is he the slave to machinery? Because he is the slave to the system for whose existence the invention of machinery was necessary.

And now I must drop, or rather have dropped, the assumption of the equality of condition, and remind you that, though in a sense we are all the slaves of machinery, yet that some men are so directly without any metaphor at all, and that these are just those on whom the great body of the arts depends—the workmen. It is necessary for the system which keeps them in their position as an inferior class that they should either be themselves machines or be the servants to machines, in no case having any interest in the work which they turn out. To their employers they are, so far as they are workmen, a part of the machinery of the workshop or the factory; to themselves they are proletarians, human beings working to live that they may live to work: their part of craftsmen, of makers of things by their own free will, is played out.

At the risk of being accused of sentimentality, I will say that since this is so, since the work which produces the things that should be matters of art is but a burden and a slavery, I exult in this at least, that it cannot produce art; that all it can do lies between stark utilitarianism and idiotic sham.

Or indeed is that merely sentimental? Rather, I think, we who have learned to see the connection between industrial slavery and the degradation of the arts have learned also to hope for a future for those arts; since the day will certainly come when men will shake off the yoke, and refuse to accept the mere artificial compulsion of the gambling market to waste their lives in ceaseless and hopeless toil; and when it does come, their instincts for beauty and imagination set free along with them, will produce such art as they need; and who can say that it will not as far surpass the art of past ages as that does the poor relics of it left us by the age of commerce?

A word or two on an objection which has often been made to me when I have been talking on this subject. It may be said, and is often, You regret the art of the Middle Ages (as indeed I do), but those who produced it were not free; they were serfs, or gild-craftsmen surrounded by brazen walls of trade restrictions; they had no political rights, and were exploited by their masters, the noble caste, most grievously. Well, I quite admit that the oppression and violence of the Middle Ages had its effect on the art of those days, its shortcomings are traceable to them; they repressed art in certain directions, I do not doubt that; and for that reason I say, that when we shake off the present oppression as we shook off the old, we may expect the art of the days of real freedom to rise above that of those old violent days. But I do say that it was possible then to have social, organic, hopeful progressive art; whereas now such poor scraps of it as are left are the result of individual and wasteful struggle, are retrospective and pessimistic. And this hopeful art was possible amidst all the oppression of those days, because the instruments of that oppression were grossly obvious, and were external to the work of the craftsman. They were laws and customs obviously intended to rob him, and open violence of the highway-robbery kind. In short, industrial production was not the instrument used for robbing the "lower classes;" it is now the main instrument used in that honourable profession. The mediæval craftsman was free in his work, therefore he made it as amusing to himself as he could; and it was his pleasure and not his pain that made all things beautiful that were made, and lavished treasures of human hope and thought on everything that man made, from a cathedral to a porridge-pot. Come, let us put it in the way least respectful to the mediæval craftsman, most polite to the modern "hand:" the poor devil of the fourteenth century, his work was of so little value that he was allowed to waste it by the hour in pleasing himself—and others; but our highly-strung mechanic, his minutes are too rich with the burden of perpetual profit for him to be allowed to waste one of them on art; the present system will not allow him—cannot allow him—to produce works of art.

So that there has arisen this strange phenomenon, that there is now a class of ladies and gentlemen, very refined indeed, though not perhaps as well informed as is generally supposed, and of this refined class there are many who do really love beauty and incident—i.e., art, and would make sacrifices to get it; and these are led by artists of great manual skill and high intellect, forming altogether a large body of demand for the article. And yet the supply does not come. Yes, and moreover, this great body of enthusiastic demanders are no mere poor and helpless people, ignorant fisher-peasants, half-mad monks, scatter-brained sansculottes—none of those, in short, the expression of whose needs has shaken the world so often before, and will do yet again. No, they are of the ruling classes, the masters of men, who can live without labour, and have abundant leisure to scheme out the fulfilment of their desires; and yet I say they cannot have the art which they so much long for, though they hunt it about the world so hard, sentimentalizing the sordid lives of the miserable peasants of Italy and the starving proletarians of her towns, now that all the picturesqueness has departed from the poor devils of our own country-side, and of our own slums. Indeed, there is little of reality left them anywhere, and that little is fast fading away before the needs of the manufacturer and his ragged regiment of workers, and before the enthusiasm of the archæological restorer of the dead past. Soon there will be nothing left except the lying dreams of history, the miserable wreckage of our museums and picture-galleries, and the carefully guarded interiors of our æsthetic drawing-rooms, unreal and foolish, fitting witnesses of the life of corruption that goes on there, so pinched and meagre and cowardly, with its concealment and ignoring, rather than restraint of, natural longings; which does not forbid the greedy indulgence in them if it can but be decently hidden.

The art then is gone, and can no more be "restored" on its old lines than a mediæval building can be. The rich and refined cannot have it though they would, and though we will believe many of them would. And why? Because those who could give it to the rich are not allowed by the rich to do so. In one word, slavery lies between us and art.

I have said as much as that the aim of art was to destroy the curse of labour by making work the pleasurable satisfaction of our impulse towards energy, and giving to that energy hope of producing something worth its exercise.

Now, therefore, I say, that since we cannot have art by striving after its mere superficial manifestation, since we can have nothing but its sham by so doing, there yet remains for us to see how it would be if we let the shadow take care of itself and try, if we can, to lay hold of the substance. For my part I believe, that if we try to realize the aims of art without much troubling ourselves what the aspect of the art itself shall be, we shall find we shall have what we want at last: whether it is to be called art or not, it will at least be life; and, after all, that is what we want. It may lead us into new splendours and beauties of visible art; to architecture with manifolded magnificence free from the curious incompleteness and failings of that which the older times have produced—to painting, uniting to the beauty which mediæval art attained the realism which modern art aims at; to sculpture, uniting the beauty of the Greek and the expression of the Renaissance with some third quality yet undiscovered, so as to give us the images of men and women splendidly alive, yet not disqualified from making, as all true sculpture should, architectural ornament. All this it may do; or, on the other hand, it may lead us into the desert, and art may seem to be dead amidst us; or feebly and uncertainly to be struggling in a world which has utterly forgotten its old glories.

For my part, with art as it now is, I cannot bring myself to think that it much matters which of these dooms awaits it, so long as each bears with it some hope of what is to come; since here, as in other matters, there is no hope save in Revolution. The old art is no longer fertile, no longer yields us anything save elegantly poetical regrets; being barren, it has but to die, and the matter of moment now is, as to how it shall die, whether with hope or without it.

What is it, for instance, that has destroyed the Rouen, the Oxford of my elegant poetic regret? Has it perished for the benefit of the people, either slowly yielding to the growth of intelligent change and new happiness? or has it been, as it were, thunderstricken by the tragedy which mostly accompanies some great new birth? Not so. Neither phalangstere nor dynamite has swept its beauty away, its destroyers have not been either the philanthropist or the Socialist, the co-operator or the anarchist. It has been sold, and at a cheap price indeed: muddled away by the greed and incompetence of fools who do not know what life and pleasure mean, who will neither take them themselves nor let others have them. That is why the death of that beauty wounds us so: no man of sense or feeling would dare to regret such losses if they had been paid for by new life and happiness for the people. But there is the people still as it was before, still facing for its part the monster who destroyed all that beauty, and whose name is Commercial Profit.

I repeat, that every scrap of genuine art will fall by the same hands if the matter only goes on long enough, although a sham art may be left in its place, which may very well be carried on by dilettanti fine gentlemen and ladies without any help from below; and, to speak plainly, I fear that this gibbering ghost of the real thing would satisfy a great many of those who now think themselves lovers of art; though it is not difficult to see a long vista of its degradation till it shall become at last a mere laughing-stock; that is to say, if the thing were to go on: I mean, if art were to be for ever the amusement of those whom we now call ladies and gentlemen.

But for my part I do not think it will go on long enough to reach such depths as that; and yet I should be hypocritical if I were to say that I thought that the change in the basis of society, which would enfranchise labour and make men practically equal in condition, would lead us by a short road to the splendid new birth of art which I have mentioned, though I feel quite certain that it would not leave what we now call art untouched, since the aims of that revolution do include the aims of art—viz., abolishing the curse of labour.

I suppose that this is what is likely to happen; that machinery will go on developing, with the purpose of saving men labour, till the mass of the people attain real leisure enough to be able to appreciate the pleasure of life; till, in fact, they have attained such mastery over Nature that they no longer fear starvation as a penalty for not working more than enough. When they get to that point they will doubtless turn themselves and begin to find out what it is that they really want to do. They would soon find out that the less work they did (the less work unaccompanied by art, I mean), the more desirable a dwelling-place the earth would be; they would accordingly do less and less work, till the mood of energy, of which I began by speaking, urged them on afresh: but by that time Nature, relieved by the relaxation of man's work, would be recovering her ancient beauty, and be teaching men the old story of art. And as the Artificial Famine, caused by men working for the profit of a master, and which we now look upon as a matter of course, would have long disappeared, they would be free to do as they chose, and they would set aside their machines in all cases where the work seemed pleasant or desirable for handiwork; till in all crafts where production of beauty was required, the most direct communication between a man's hand and his brain would be sought for. And there would be many occupations also, as the processes of agriculture, in which the voluntary exercise of energy would be thought so delightful, that people would not dream of handing over its pleasure to the jaws of a machine.

In short, men will find out that the men of our days were wrong in first multiplying their needs, and then trying, each man of them, to evade all participation in the means and processes whereby those needs are satisfied; that this kind of division of labour is really only a new and wilful form of arrogant and slothful ignorance, far more injurious to the happiness and contentment of life than the ignorance of the processes of Nature, of what we sometimes call science, which men of the earlier days unwittingly lived in.

They will discover, or rediscover rather, that the true secret of happiness lies in the taking a genuine interest in all the details of daily life, in elevating them by art instead of handing the performance of them over to unregarded drudges, and ignoring them; and that in cases where it was impossible either so to elevate them and make them interesting, or to lighten them by the use of machinery, so as to make the labour of them trifling, that should be taken as a token that the supposed advantages gained by them were not worth the trouble and had better be given up. All this to my mind would be the outcome of men throwing off the burden of Artificial Famine, supposing, as I cannot help supposing, that the impulses which have from the first glimmerings of history urged men on to the practice of Art were still at work in them.

Thus and thus only can come about the new birth of Art, and I think it will come about thus. You may say it is a long process, and so it is; but I can conceive of a longer. I have given you the Socialist or Optimist view of the matter. Now for the Pessimist view.

I can conceive that the revolt against Artificial Famine or Capitalism, which is now on foot, may be vanquished. The result will be that the working class—the slaves of society—will become more and more degraded; that they will not strive against overwhelming force, but, stimulated by that love of life which Nature, always anxious about the perpetuation of the race, has implanted in us, will learn to bear everything—starvation, overwork, dirt, ignorance, brutality. All these things they will bear, as, alas! they bear them too well even now; all this rather than risk sweet life and bitter livelihood, and all sparks of hope and manliness will die out of them.

Nor will their masters be much better off: the earth's surface will be hideous everywhere, save in the uninhabitable desert; Art will utterly perish, as in the manual arts so in literature, which will become, as it is indeed speedily becoming, a mere string of orderly and calculated ineptitudes and passionless ingenuities; Science will grow more and more one-sided, more incomplete, more wordy and useless, till at last she will pile herself up into such a mass of superstition, that beside it the theologies of old time will seem mere reason and enlightenment. All will get lower and lower, till the heroic struggles of the past to realize hope from year to year, from century to century, will be utterly forgotten, and man will be an indescribable being—hopeless, desireless, lifeless.

And will there be deliverance from this even? Maybe: man may, after some terrible cataclysm, learn to strive towards a healthy animalism, may grow from a tolerable animal into a savage, from a savage into a barbarian, and so on; and some thousands of years hence he may be beginning once more those arts which we have now lost, and be carving interlacements like the New Zealanders, or scratching forms of animals on their cleaned blade-bones, like the pre-historic men of the drift.

But in any case, according to the pessimist view, which looks upon revolt against Artificial Famine as impossible to succeed, we shall wearily trudge the circle again, until some accident, some unforeseen consequence of arrangement, makes an end of us altogether.

That pessimism I do not believe in, nor, on the other hand, do I suppose that it is altogether a matter of our wills as to whether we shall further human progress or human degradation; yet, since there are those who are impelled towards the Socialist or Optimistic side of things, I must conclude that there is some hope of its prevailing, that the strenuous efforts of many individuals imply a force which is thrusting them on. So that I believe that the "Aims of Art" will be realized, though I know that they cannot be, so long as we groan under the tyranny of Artificial Famine. Once again I warn you against supposing, you who may specially love art, that you will do any good by attempting to revivify art by dealing with its dead exterior. I say it is the aims of art that you must seek rather than the art itself; and in that search we may find ourselves in a world blank and bare, as the result of our caring at least this much for art, that we will not endure the shams of it.

Anyhow, I ask you to think with me that the worst which can happen to us is to endure tamely the evils that we see; that no trouble or turmoil is so bad as that; that the necessary destruction which reconstruction bears with it must be taken calmly; that everywhere—in State, in Church, in the household—we must be resolute to endure no tyranny, accept no lie, quail before no fear, although they may come before us disguised as piety, duty, or affection, as useful opportunity and good-nature, as prudence or kindness. The world's roughness, falseness, and injustice will bring about their natural consequences, and we and our lives are part of those consequences; but since we inherit also the consequences of old resistance to those curses, let us each look to it to have our fair share of that inheritance also, which, if nothing else come of it, will at least bring to us courage and hope; that is, eager life while we live, which is above all things the Aim of Art.

USEFUL WORK VERSUS USELESS TOIL.

The above title may strike some of my readers as strange. It is assumed by most people nowadays that all work is useful, and by most well-to-to people that all work is desirable. Most people, well-to-do or not, believe that, even when a man is doing work which appears to be useless, he is earning his livelihood by it—he is "employed," as the phrase goes; and most of those who are well-to-do cheer on the happy worker with congratulations and praises, if he is only "industrious" enough and deprives himself of all pleasure and holidays in the sacred cause of labour. In short, it has become an article of the creed of modern morality that all labour is good in itself—a convenient belief to those who live on the labour of others. But as to those on whom they live, I recommend them not to take it on trust, but to look into the matter a little deeper.

Let us grant, first, that the race of man must either labour or perish. Nature does not give us our livelihood gratis; we must win it by toil of some sort or degree. Let us see, then, if she does not give us some compensation for this compulsion to labour, since certainly in other matters she takes care to make the acts necessary to the continuance of life in the individual and the race not only endurable, but even pleasurable.

You may be sure that she does so, that it is of the nature of man, when he is not diseased, to take pleasure in his work under certain conditions. And, yet, we must say in the teeth of the hypocritical praise of all labour, whatsoever it may be, of which I have made mention, that there is some labour which is so far from being a blessing that it is a curse; that it would be better for the community and for the worker if the latter were to fold his hands and refuse to work, and either die or let us pack him off to the workhouse or prison—which you will.

Here, you see, are two kinds of work—one good, the other bad; one not far removed from a blessing, a lightening of life; the other a mere curse, a burden to life.

What is the difference between them, then? This: one has hope in it, the other has not. It is manly to do the one kind of work, and manly also to refuse to do the other.

What is the nature of the hope which, when it is present in work, makes it worth doing?

It is threefold, I think—hope of rest, hope of product, hope of pleasure in the work itself; and hope of these also in some abundance and of good quality; rest enough and good enough to be worth having; product worth having by one who is neither a fool nor an ascetic; pleasure enough for all for us to be conscious of it while we are at work; not a mere habit, the loss of which we shall feel as a fidgety man feels the loss of the bit of string he fidgets with.

I have put the hope of rest first because it is the simplest and most natural part of our hope. Whatever pleasure there is in some work, there is certainly some pain in all work, the beast-like pain of stirring up our slumbering energies to action, the beast-like dread of change when things are pretty well with us; and the compensation for this animal pain is animal rest. We must feel while we are working that the time will come when we shall not have to work. Also the rest, when it comes, must be long enough to allow us to enjoy it; it must be longer than is merely necessary for us to recover the strength we have expended in working, and it must be animal rest also in this, that it must not be disturbed by anxiety, else we shall not be able to enjoy it. If we have this amount and kind of rest we shall, so far, be no worse off than the beasts.

As to the hope of product, I have said that Nature compels us to work for that. It remains for us to look to it that we do really produce something, and not nothing, or at least nothing that we want or are allowed to use. If we look to this and use our wills we shall, so far, be better than machines.

The hope of pleasure in the work itself: how strange that hope must seem to some of my readers—to most of them! Yet I think that to all living things there is a pleasure in the exercise of their energies, and that even beasts rejoice in being lithe and swift and strong. But a man at work, making something which he feels will exist because he is working at it and wills it, is exercising the energies of his mind and soul as well as of his body. Memory and imagination help him as he works. Not only his own thoughts, but the thoughts of the men of past ages guide his hands; and, as a part of the human race, he creates. If we work thus we shall be men, and our days will be happy and eventful.

Thus worthy work carries with it the hope of pleasure in rest, the hope of the pleasure in our using what it makes, and the hope of pleasure in our daily creative skill.

All other work but this is worthless; it is slaves' work—mere toiling to live, that we may live to toil.

Therefore, since we have, as it were, a pair of scales in which to weigh the work now done in the world, let us use them. Let us estimate the worthiness of the work we do, after so many thousand years of toil, so many promises of hope deferred, such boundless exultation over the progress of civilization and the gain of liberty.

Now, the first thing as to the work done in civilization and the easiest to notice is that it is portioned out very unequally amongst the different classes of society. First, there are people—not a few—who do no work, and make no pretence of doing any. Next, there are people, and very many of them, who work fairly hard, though with abundant easements and holidays, claimed and allowed; and lastly, there are people who work so hard that they may be said to do nothing else than work, and are accordingly called "the working classes," as distinguished from the middle classes and the rich, or aristocracy, whom I have mentioned above.

It is clear that this inequality presses heavily upon the "working" class, and must visibly tend to destroy their hope of rest at least, and so, in that particular, make them worse off than mere beasts of the field; but that is not the sum and end of our folly of turning useful work into useless toil, but only the beginning of it.

For first, as to the class of rich people doing no work, we all know that they consume a great deal while they produce nothing. Therefore, clearly, they have to be kept at the expense of those who do work, just as paupers have, and are a mere burden on the community. In these days there are many who have learned to see this, though they can see no further into the evils of our present system, and have formed no idea of any scheme for getting rid of this burden; though perhaps they have a vague hope that changes in the system of voting for members of the House of Commons may, as if by magic, tend in that direction. With such hopes or superstitions we need not trouble ourselves. Moreover, this class, the aristocracy, once thought most necessary to the State, is scant of numbers, and has now no power of its own, but depends on the support of the class next below it—the middle class. In fact, it is really composed either of the most successful men of that class, or of their immediate descendants.

As to the middle class, including the trading, manufacturing, and professional people of our society, they do, as a rule, seem to work quite hard enough, and so at first sight might be thought to help the community, and not burden it. But by far the greater part of them, though they work, do not produce, and even when they do produce, as in the case of those engaged (wastefully indeed) in the distribution of goods, or doctors, or (genuine) artists and literary men, they consume out of all proportion to their due share. The commercial and manufacturing part of them, the most powerful part, spend their lives and energies in fighting amongst themselves for their respective shares of the wealth which they force the genuine workers to provide for them; the others are almost wholly the hangers-on of these; they do not work for the public, but a privileged class: they are the parasites of property, sometimes, as in the case of lawyers, undisguisedly so; sometimes, as the doctors and others above mentioned, professing to be useful, but too often of no use save as supporters of the system of folly, fraud, and tyranny of which they form a part. And all these we must remember have, as a rule, one aim in view; not the production of utilities, but the gaining of a position either for themselves or their children in which they will not have to work at all. It is their ambition and the end of their whole lives to gain, if not for themselves yet at least for their children, the proud position of being obvious burdens on the community. For their work itself in spite of the sham dignity with which they surround it, they care nothing: save a few enthusiasts, men of science, art or letters, who, if they are not the salt of the earth, are at least (and oh, the pity of it!) the salt of the miserable system of which they are the slaves, which hinders and thwarts them at every turn, and even sometimes corrupts them.

Here then is another class, this time very numerous and all-powerful, which produces very little and consumes enormously, and is therefore in the main supported, as paupers are, by the real producers. The class that remains to be considered produces all that is produced, and supports both itself and the other classes, though it is placed in a position of inferiority to them; real inferiority, mind you, involving a degradation both of mind and body. But it is a necessary consequence of this tyranny and folly that again many of these workers are not producers. A vast number of them once more are merely parasites of property, some of them openly so, as the soldiers by land and sea who are kept on foot for the perpetuating of national rivalries and enmities, and for the purposes of the national struggle for the share of the product of unpaid labour. But besides this obvious burden on the producers and the scarcely less obvious one of domestic servants, there is first the army of clerks, shop-assistants, and so forth, who are engaged in the service of the private war for wealth, which, as above said, is the real occupation of the well-to-do middle class. This is a larger body of workers than might be supposed, for it includes amongst others all those engaged in what I should call competitive salesmanship, or, to use a less dignified word, the puffery of wares, which has now got to such a pitch that there are many things which cost far more to sell than they do to make.

Next there is the mass of people employed in making all those articles of folly and luxury, the demand for which is the outcome of the existence of the rich non-producing classes; things which people leading a manly and uncorrupted life would not ask for or dream of. These things, whoever may gainsay me, I will for ever refuse to call wealth: they are not wealth, but waste. Wealth is what Nature gives us and what a reasonable man can make out of the gifts of Nature for his reasonable use. The sunlight, the fresh air, the unspoiled face of the earth, food, raiment and housing necessary and decent; the storing up of knowledge of all kinds, and the power of disseminating it; means of free communication between man and man; works of art, the beauty which man creates when he is most a man, most aspiring and thoughtful—all things which serve the pleasure of people, free, manly and uncorrupted. This is wealth. Nor can I think of anything worth having which does not come under one or other of these heads. But think, I beseech you, of the product of England, the workshop of the world, and will you not be bewildered, as I am, at the thought of the mass of things which no sane man could desire, but which our useless toil makes—and sells?

Now, further, there is even a sadder industry yet, which is forced on many, very many, of our workers—the making of wares which are necessary to them and their brethren, because they are an inferior class. For if many men live without producing, nay, must live lives so empty and foolish that they force a great part of the workers to produce wares which no one needs, not even the rich, it follows that most men must be poor; and, living as they do on wages from those whom they support, cannot get for their use the goods which men naturally desire, but must put up with miserable makeshifts for them, with coarse food that does not nourish, with rotten raiment which does not shelter, with wretched houses which may well make a town-dweller in civilization look back with regret to the tent of the nomad tribe, or the cave of the pre-historic savage. Nay, the workers must even lend a hand to the great industrial invention of the age—adulteration, and by its help produce for their own use shams and mockeries of the luxury of the rich; for the wage-earners must always live as the wage-payers bid them, and their very habits of life are forced on them by their masters.

But it is waste of time to try to express in words due contempt of the productions of the much-praised cheapness of our epoch. It must be enough to say that this cheapness is necessary to the system of exploiting on which modern manufacture rests. In other words, our society includes a great mass of slaves, who must be fed, clothed, housed and amused as slaves, and that their daily necessity compels them to make the slave-wares whose use is the perpetuation of their slavery.

To sum up, then, concerning the manner of work in civilized States, these States are composed of three classes—a class which does not even pretend to work, a class which pretends to work but which produces nothing, and a class which works, but is compelled by the other two classes to do work which is often unproductive.

Civilization therefore wastes its own resources, and will do so as long as the present system lasts. These are cold words with which to describe the tyranny under which we suffer; try then to consider what they mean.

There is a certain amount of natural material and of natural forces in the world, and a certain amount of labour-power inherent in the persons of the men that inhabit it. Men urged by their necessities and desires have laboured for many thousands of years at the task of subjugating the forces of Nature and of making the natural material useful to them. To our eyes, since we cannot see into the future, that struggle with Nature seems nearly over, and the victory of the human race over her nearly complete. And, looking backwards to the time when history first began, we note that the progress of that victory has been far swifter and more startling within the last two hundred years than ever before. Surely, therefore, we moderns ought to be in all ways vastly better off than any who have gone before us. Surely we ought, one and all of us, to be wealthy, to be well furnished with the good things which our victory over Nature has won for us.

But what is the real fact? Who will dare to deny that the great mass of civilized men are poor? So poor are they that it is mere childishness troubling ourselves to discuss whether perhaps they are in some ways a little better off than their forefathers. They are poor; nor can their poverty be measured by the poverty of a resourceless savage, for he knows of nothing else than his poverty; that he should be cold, hungry, houseless, dirty, ignorant, all that is to him as natural as that he should have a skin. But for us, for the most of us, civilization has bred desires which she forbids us to satisfy, and so is not merely a niggard but a torturer also.

Thus then have the fruits of our victory over Nature been stolen from us, thus has compulsion by Nature to labour in hope of rest, gain, and pleasure been turned into compulsion by man to labour in hope—of living to labour!

What shall we do then, can we mend it?

Well, remember once more that it is not our remote ancestors who achieved the victory over Nature, but our fathers, nay, our very selves. For us to sit hopeless and helpless then would be a strange folly indeed: be sure that we can amend it. What, then, is the first thing to be done?

We have seen that modern society is divided into two classes, one of which is privileged to be kept by the labour of the other—that is, it forces the other to work for it and takes from this inferior class everything that it can take from it, and uses the wealth so taken to keep its own members in a superior position, to make them beings of a higher order than the others: longer lived, more beautiful, more honoured, more refined than those of the other class. I do not say that it troubles itself about its members being positively long lived, beautiful or refined, but merely insists that they shall be so relatively to the inferior class. As also it cannot use the labour-power of the inferior class fairly in producing real wealth, it wastes it wholesale in the production of rubbish.

It is this robbery and waste on the part of the minority which keeps the majority poor; if it could be shown that it is necessary for the preservation of society that this should be submitted to, little more could be said on the matter, save that the despair of the oppressed majority would probably at some time or other destroy Society. But it has been shown, on the contrary, even by such incomplete experiments, for instance, as Co-operation (so called), that the existence of a privileged class is by no means necessary for the production of wealth, but rather for the "government" of the producers of wealth, or, in other words, for the upholding of privilege.

The first step to be taken then is to abolish a class of men privileged to shirk their duties as men, thus forcing others to do the work which they refuse to do. All must work according to their ability, and so produce what they consume—that is, each man should work as well as he can for his own livelihood, and his livelihood should be assured to him; that is to say, all the advantages which society would provide for each and all of its members.

Thus, at last, would true Society be founded. It would rest on equality of condition. No man would be tormented for the benefit of another—nay, no one man would be tormented for the benefit of Society. Nor, indeed, can that order be called Society which is not upheld for the benefit of every one of its members.

But since men live now, badly as they live, when so many people do not produce at all, and when so much work is wasted, it is clear that, under conditions where all produced and no work was wasted, not only would every one work with the certain hope of gaining a due share of wealth by his work, but also he could not miss his due share of rest. Here, then, are two out of the three kinds of hope mentioned above as an essential part of worthy work assured to the worker. When class robbery is abolished, every man will reap the fruits of his labour, every man will have due rest—leisure, that is. Some Socialists might say we need not go any further than this; it is enough that the worker should get the full produce of his work, and that his rest should be abundant. But though the compulsion of man's tyranny is thus abolished, I yet demand compensation for the compulsion of Nature's necessity. As long as the work is repulsive it will still be a burden which must be taken up daily, and even so would mar our life, even though the hours of labour were short. What we want to do is to add to our wealth without diminishing our pleasure. Nature will not be finally conquered till our work becomes a part of the pleasure of our lives.

That first step of freeing people from the compulsion to labour needlessly will at least put us on the way towards this happy end; for we shall then have time and opportunities for bringing it about. As things are now, between the waste of labour-power in mere idleness and its waste in unproductive work, it is clear that the world of civilization is supported by a small part of its people; when all were working usefully for its support, the share of work which each would have to do would be but small, if our standard of life were about on the footing of what well-to-do and refined people now think desirable. We shall have labour-power to spare, and shall, in short, be as wealthy as we please. It will be easy to live. If we were to wake up some morning now, under our present system, and find it "easy to live," that system would force us to set to work at once and make it hard to live; we should call that "developing our resources," or some such fine name. The multiplication of labour has become a necessity for us, and as long as that goes on no ingenuity in the invention of machines will be of any real use to us. Each new machine will cause a certain amount of misery among the workers whose special industry it may disturb; so many of them will be reduced from skilled to unskilled workmen, and then gradually matters will slip into their due grooves, and all will work apparently smoothly again; and if it were not that all this is preparing revolution, things would be, for the greater part of men, just as they were before the new wonderful invention.

But when revolution has made it "easy to live," when all are working harmoniously together and there is no one to rob the worker of his time, that is to say, his life; in those coming days there will be no compulsion on us to go on producing things we do not want, no compulsion on us to labour for nothing; we shall be able calmly and thoughtfully to consider what we shall do with our wealth of labour-power. Now, for my part, I think the first use we ought to make of that wealth, of that freedom, should be to make all our labour, even the commonest and most necessary, pleasant to everybody; for thinking over the matter carefully I can see that the one course which will certainly make life happy in the face of all accidents and troubles is to take a pleasurable interest in all the details of life. And lest perchance you think that an assertion too universally accepted to be worth making, let me remind you how entirely modern civilization forbids it; with what sordid, and even terrible, details it surrounds the life of the poor, what a mechanical and empty life she forces on the rich; and how rare a holiday it is for any of us to feel ourselves a part of Nature, and unhurriedly, thoughtfully, and happily to note the course of our lives amidst all the little links of events which connect them with the lives of others, and build up the great whole of humanity.

But such a holiday our whole lives might be, if we were resolute to make all our labour reasonable and pleasant. But we must be resolute indeed; for no half measures will help us here. It has been said already that our present joyless labour, and our lives scared and anxious as the life of a hunted beast, are forced upon us by the present system of producing for the profit of the privileged classes. It is necessary to state what this means. Under the present system of wages and capital the "manufacturer" (most absurdly so called, since a manufacturer means a person who makes with his hands) having a monopoly of the means whereby the power to labour inherent in every man's body can be used for production, is the master of those who are not so privileged; he, and he alone, is able to make use of this labour-power, which, on the other hand, is the only commodity by means of which his "capital," that is to say, the accumulated product of past labour, can be made productive to him. He therefore buys the labour-power of those who are bare of capital and can only live by selling it to him; his purpose in this transaction is to increase his capital, to make it breed. It is clear that if he paid those with whom he makes his bargain the full value of their labour, that is to say, all that they produced, he would fail in his purpose. But since he is the monopolist of the means of productive labour, he can compel them to make a bargain better for him and worse for them than that; which bargain is that after they have earned their livelihood, estimated according to a standard high enough to ensure their peaceable submission to his mastership, the rest (and by far the larger part as a matter of fact) of what they produce shall belong to him, shall be his property to do as he likes with, to use or abuse at his pleasure; which property is, as we all know, jealously guarded by army and navy, police and prison; in short, by that huge mass of physical force which superstition, habit, fear of death by starvation—Ignorance, in one word, among the propertyless masses enables the propertied classes to use for the subjection of—their slaves.

Now, at other times, other evils resulting from this system may be put forward. What I want to point out now is the impossibility of our attaining to attractive labour under this system, and to repeat that it is this robbery (there is no other word for it) which wastes the available labour-power of the civilized world, forcing many men to do nothing, and many, very many more to do nothing useful; and forcing those who carry on really useful labour to most burdensome over-work. For understand once for all that the "manufacturer" aims primarily at producing, by means of the labour he has stolen from others, not goods but profits, that is, the "wealth" that is produced over and above the livelihood of his workmen, and the wear and tear of his machinery. Whether that "wealth" is real or sham matters nothing to him. If it sells and yields him a "profit" it is all right. I have said that, owing to there being rich people who have more money than they can spend reasonably, and who therefore buy sham wealth, there is waste on that side; and also that, owing to there being poor people who cannot afford to buy things which are worth making, there is waste on that side. So that the "demand" which the capitalist "supplies" is a false demand. The market in which he sells is "rigged" by the miserable inequalities produced by the robbery of the system of Capital and Wages.

It is this system, therefore, which we must be resolute in getting rid of, if we are to attain to happy and useful work for all. The first step towards making labour attractive is to get the means of making labour fruitful, the Capital, including the land, machinery, factories, &c., into the hands of the community, to be used for the good of all alike, so that we might all work at "supplying" the real "demands" of each and all—that is to say, work for livelihood, instead of working to supply the demand of the profit market—instead of working for profit—i.e., the power of compelling other men to work against their will.

When this first step has been taken and men begin to understand that Nature wills all men either to work or starve, and when they are no longer such fools as to allow some the alternative of stealing, when this happy day is come, we shall then be relieved from the tax of waste, and consequently shall find that we have, as aforesaid, a mass of labour-power available, which will enable us to live as we please within reasonable limits. We shall no longer be hurried and driven by the fear of starvation, which at present presses no less on the greater part of men in civilized communities than it does on mere savages. The first and most obvious necessities will be so easily provided for in a community in which there is no waste of labour, that we shall have time to look round and consider what we really do want, that can be obtained without over-taxing our energies; for the often-expressed fear of mere idleness falling upon us when the force supplied by the present hierarchy of compulsion is withdrawn, is a fear which is but generated by the burden of excessive and repulsive labour, which we most of us have to bear at present.

I say once more that, in my belief, the first thing which we shall think so necessary as to be worth sacrificing some idle time for, will be the attractiveness of labour. No very heavy sacrifice will be required for attaining this object, but some will be required. For we may hope that men who have just waded through a period of strife and revolution will be the last to put up long with a life of mere utilitarianism, though Socialists are sometimes accused by ignorant persons of aiming at such a life. On the other hand, the ornamental part of modern life is already rotten to the core, and must be utterly swept away before the new order of things is realized. There is nothing of it—there is nothing which could come of it that could satisfy the aspirations of men set free from the tyranny of commercialism.

We must begin to build up the ornamental part of life—its pleasures, bodily and mental, scientific and artistic, social and individual—on the basis of work undertaken willingly and cheerfully, with the consciousness of benefiting ourselves and our neighbours by it. Such absolutely necessary work as we should have to do would in the first place take up but a small part of each day, and so far would not be burdensome; but it would be a task of daily recurrence, and therefore would spoil our day's pleasure unless it were made at least endurable while it lasted. In other words, all labour, even the commonest, must be made attractive.

How can this be done?—is the question the answer to which will take up the rest of this paper. In giving some hints on this question, I know that, while all Socialists will agree with many of the suggestions made, some of them may seem to some strange and venturesome. These must be considered as being given without any intention of dogmatizing, and as merely expressing my own personal opinion.

From all that has been said already it follows that labour, to be attractive, must be directed towards some obviously useful end, unless in cases where it is undertaken voluntarily by each individual as a pastime. This element of obvious usefulness is all the more to be counted on in sweetening tasks otherwise irksome, since social morality, the responsibility of man towards the life of man, will, in the new order of things, take the place of theological morality, or the responsibility of man to some abstract idea. Next, the day's work will be short. This need not be insisted on. It is clear that with work unwasted it can be short. It is clear also that much work which is now a torment, would be easily endurable if it were much shortened.

Variety of work is the next point, and a most important one. To compel a man to do day after day the same task, without any hope of escape or change, means nothing short of turning his life into a prison-torment. Nothing but the tyranny of profit-grinding makes this necessary. A man might easily learn and practise at least three crafts, varying sedentary occupation with outdoor—occupation calling for the exercise of strong bodily energy for work in which the mind had more to do. There are few men, for instance, who would not wish to spend part of their lives in the most necessary and pleasantest of all work—cultivating the earth. One thing which will make this variety of employment possible will be the form that education will take in a socially ordered community. At present all education is directed towards the end of fitting people to take their places in the hierarchy of commerce—these as masters, those as workmen. The education of the masters is more ornamental than that of the workmen, but it is commercial still; and even at the ancient universities learning is but little regarded, unless it can in the long run be made to pay. Due education is a totally different thing from this, and concerns itself in finding out what different people are fit for, and helping them along the road which they are inclined to take. In a duly ordered society, therefore, young people would be taught such handicrafts as they had a turn for as a part of their education, the discipline of their minds and bodies; and adults would also have opportunities of learning in the same schools, for the development of individual capacities would be of all things chiefly aimed at by education, instead, as now, the subordination of all capacities to the great end of "money-making" for oneself—or one's master. The amount of talent, and even genius, which the present system crushes, and which would be drawn out by such a system, would make our daily work easy and interesting.

Under this head of variety I will note one product of industry which has suffered so much from commercialism that it can scarcely be said to exist, and is, indeed, so foreign from our epoch that I fear there are some who will find it difficult to understand what I have to say on the subject, which I nevertheless must say, since it is really a most important one. I mean that side of art which is, or ought to be, done by the ordinary workman while he is about his ordinary work, and which has got to be called, very properly, Popular Art. This art, I repeat, no longer exists now, having been killed by commercialism. But from the beginning of man's contest with Nature till the rise of the present capitalistic system, it was alive, and generally flourished. While it lasted, everything that was made by man was adorned by man, just as everything made by Nature is adorned by her. The craftsman, as he fashioned the thing he had under his hand, ornamented it so naturally and so entirely without conscious effort, that it is often difficult to distinguish where the mere utilitarian part of his work ended and the ornamental began. Now the origin of this art was the necessity that the workman felt for variety in his work, and though the beauty produced by this desire was a great gift to the world, yet the obtaining variety and pleasure in the work by the workman was a matter of more importance still, for it stamped all labour with the impress of pleasure. All this has now quite disappeared from the work of civilization. If you wish to have ornament, you must pay specially for it, and the workman is compelled to produce ornament, as he is to produce other wares. He is compelled to pretend happiness in his work, so that the beauty produced by man's hand, which was once a solace to his labour, has now become an extra burden to him, and ornament is now but one of the follies of useless toil, and perhaps not the least irksome of its fetters.

Besides the short duration of labour, its conscious usefulness, and the variety which should go with it, there is another thing needed to make it attractive, and that is pleasant surroundings. The misery and squalor which we people of civilization bear with so much complacency as a necessary part of the manufacturing system, is just as necessary to the community at large as a proportionate amount of filth would be in the house of a private rich man. If such a man were to allow the cinders to be raked all over his drawing-room, and a privy to be established in each corner of his dining-room, if he habitually made a dust and refuse heap of his once beautiful garden, never washed his sheets or changed his tablecloth, and made his family sleep five in a bed, he would surely find himself in the claws of a commission de lunatico. But such acts of miserly folly are just what our present society is doing daily under the compulsion of a supposed necessity, which is nothing short of madness. I beg you to bring your commission of lunacy against civilization without more delay.

For all our crowded towns and bewildering factories are simply the outcome of the profit system. Capitalistic manufacture, capitalistic land-owning, and capitalistic exchange force men into big cities in order to manipulate them in the interests of capital; the same tyranny contracts the due space of the factory so much that (for instance) the interior of a great weaving-shed is almost as ridiculous a spectacle as it is a horrible one. There is no other necessity for all this, save the necessity for grinding profits out of men's lives, and of producing cheap goods for the use (and subjection) of the slaves who grind. All labour is not yet driven into factories; often where it is there is no necessity for it, save again the profit-tyranny. People engaged in all such labour need by no means be compelled to pig together in close city quarters. There is no reason why they should not follow their occupations in quiet country homes, in industrial colleges, in small towns, or, in short, where they find it happiest for them to live.

As to that part of labour which must be associated on a large scale, this very factory system, under a reasonable order of things (though to my mind there might still be drawbacks to it), would at least offer opportunities for a full and eager social life surrounded by many pleasures. The factories might be centres of intellectual activity also, and work in them might well be varied very much: the tending of the necessary machinery might to each individual be but a short part of the day's work. The other work might vary from raising food from the surrounding country to the study and practice of art and science. It is a matter of course that people engaged in such work, and being the masters of their own lives, would not allow any hurry or want of foresight to force them into enduring dirt, disorder, or want of room. Science duly applied would enable them to get rid of refuse, to minimize, if not wholly to destroy, all the inconveniences which at present attend the use of elaborate machinery, such as smoke, stench and noise; nor would they endure that the buildings in which they worked or lived should be ugly blots on the fair face of the earth. Beginning by making their factories, buildings, and sheds decent and convenient like their homes, they would infallibly go on to make them not merely negatively good, inoffensive merely, but even beautiful, so that the glorious art of architecture, now for some time slain by commercial greed, would be born again and flourish.

So, you see, I claim that work in a duly ordered community should be made attractive by the consciousness of usefulness, by its being carried on with intelligent interest, by variety, and by its being exercised amidst pleasurable surroundings. But I have also claimed, as we all do, that the day's work should not be wearisomely long. It may be said, "How can you make this last claim square with the others? If the work is to be so refined, will not the goods made be very expensive?"

I do admit, as I have said before, that some sacrifice will be necessary in order to make labour attractive. I mean that, if we could be contented in a free community to work in the same hurried, dirty, disorderly, heartless way as we do now, we might shorten our day's labour very much more than I suppose we shall do, taking all kinds of labour into account. But if we did, it would mean that our new-won freedom of condition would leave us listless and wretched, if not anxious, as we are now, which I hold is simply impossible. We should be contented to make the sacrifices necessary for raising our condition to the standard called out for as desirable by the whole community. Nor only so. We should, individually, be emulous to sacrifice quite freely still more of our time and our ease towards the raising of the standard of life. Persons, either by themselves or associated for such purposes, would freely, and for the love of the work and for its results—stimulated by the hope of the pleasure of creation—produce those ornaments of life for the service of all, which they are now bribed to produce (or pretend to produce) for the service of a few rich men. The experiment of a civilized community living wholly without art or literature has not yet been tried. The past degradation and corruption of civilization may force this denial of pleasure upon the society which will arise from its ashes. If that must be, we will accept the passing phase of utilitarianism as a foundation for the art which is to be. If the cripple and the starveling disappear from our streets, if the earth nourish us all alike, if the sun shine for all of us alike, if to one and all of us the glorious drama of the earth—day and night, summer and winter—can be presented as a thing to understand and love, we can afford to wait awhile till we are purified from the shame of the past corruption, and till art arises again amongst people freed from the terror of the slave and the shame of the robber.

Meantime, in any case, the refinement, thoughtfulness, and deliberation of labour must indeed be paid for, but not by compulsion to labour long hours. Our epoch has invented machines which would have appeared wild dreams to the men of past ages, and of those machines we have as yet made no use.

They are called "labour-saving" machines—a commonly used phrase which implies what we expect of them; but we do not get what we expect. What they really do is to reduce the skilled labourer to the ranks of the unskilled, to increase the number of the "reserve army of labour"—that is, to increase the precariousness of life among the workers and to intensify the labour of those who serve the machines (as slaves their masters). All this they do by the way, while they pile up the profits of the employers of labour, or force them to expend those profits in bitter commercial war with each other. In a true society these miracles of ingenuity would be for the first time used for minimizing the amount of time spent in unattractive labour, which by their means might be so reduced as to be but a very light burden on each individual. All the more as these machines would most certainly be very much improved when it was no longer a question as to whether their improvement would "pay" the individual, but rather whether it would benefit the community.

So much for the ordinary use of machinery, which would probably, after a time, be somewhat restricted when men found out that there was no need for anxiety as to mere subsistence, and learned to take an interest and pleasure in handiwork which, done deliberately and thoughtfully, could be made more attractive than machine work.

Again, as people freed from the daily terror of starvation find out what they really wanted, being no longer compelled by anything but their own needs, they would refuse to produce the mere inanities which are now called luxuries, or the poison and trash now called cheap wares. No one would make plush breeches when there were no flunkies to wear them, nor would anybody waste his time over making oleomargarine when no one was compelled to abstain from real butter. Adulteration laws are only needed in a society of thieves—and in such a society they are a dead letter.

Socialists are often asked how work of the rougher and more repulsive kind could be carried out in the new condition of things. To attempt to answer such questions fully or authoritatively would be attempting the impossibility of constructing a scheme of a new society out of the materials of the old, before we knew which of those materials would disappear and which endure through the evolution which is leading us to the great change. Yet it is not difficult to conceive of some arrangement whereby those who did the roughest work should work for the shortest spells. And again, what is said above of the variety of work applies specially here. Once more I say, that for a man to be the whole of his life hopelessly engaged in performing one repulsive and never-ending task, is an arrangement fit enough for the hell imagined by theologians, but scarcely fit for any other form of society. Lastly, if this rougher work were of any special kind, we may suppose that special volunteers would be called on to perform it, who would surely be forthcoming, unless men in a state of freedom should lose the sparks of manliness which they possessed as slaves.

And yet if there be any work which cannot be made other than repulsive, either by the shortness of its duration or the intermittency of its recurrence, or by the sense of special and peculiar usefulness (and therefore honour) in the mind of the man who performs it freely,—if there be any work which cannot be but a torment to the worker, what then? Well, then, let us see if the heavens will fall on us if we leave it undone, for it were better that they should. The produce of such work cannot be worth the price of it.

Now we have seen that the semi-theological dogma that all labour, under any circumstances, is a blessing to the labourer, is hypocritical and false; that, on the other hand, labour is good when due hope of rest and pleasure accompanies it. We have weighed the work of civilization in the balance and found it wanting, since hope is mostly lacking to it, and therefore we see that civilization has bred a dire curse for men. But we have seen also that the work of the world might be carried on in hope and with pleasure if it were not wasted by folly and tyranny, by the perpetual strife of opposing classes.

It is Peace, therefore, which we need in order that we may live and work in hope and with pleasure. Peace so much desired, if we may trust men's words, but which has been so continually and steadily rejected by them in deeds. But for us, let us set our hearts on it and win it at whatever cost.

What the cost may be, who can tell? Will it be possible to win peace peaceably? Alas, how can it be? We are so hemmed in by wrong and folly, that in one way or other we must always be fighting against them: our own lives may see no end to the struggle, perhaps no obvious hope of the end. It may be that the best we can hope to see is that struggle getting sharper and bitterer day by day, until it breaks out openly at last into the slaughter of men by actual warfare instead of by the slower and crueller methods of "peaceful" commerce. If we live to see that, we shall live to see much; for it will mean the rich classes grown conscious of their own wrong and robbery, and consciously defending them by open violence; and then the end will be drawing near.

But in any case, and whatever the nature of our strife for peace may be, if we only aim at it steadily and with singleness of heart, and ever keep it in view, a reflection from that peace of the future will illumine the turmoil and trouble of our lives, whether the trouble be seemingly petty, or obviously tragic; and we shall, in our hopes at least, live the lives of men: nor can the present times give us any reward greater than that.

DAWN OF A NEW EPOCH.

Perhaps some of my readers may think that the above title is not a correct one: it may be said, a new epoch is always dawning, change is always going on, and it goes on so gradually that we do not know when we are out of an old epoch and into a new one. There is truth in that, at least to this extent, that no age can see itself: we must stand some way off before the confused picture with its rugged surface can resolve itself into its due order, and seem to be something with a definite purpose carried through all its details. Nevertheless, when we look back on history we do distinguish periods in the lapse of time that are not merely arbitrary ones, we note the early growth of the ideas which are to form the new order of things, we note their development into the transitional period, and finally the new epoch is revealed to us bearing in its full development, unseen as yet, the seeds of the newer order still which shall transform it in its turn into something else.

Moreover, there are periods in which even those alive in them become more or less conscious of the change which is always going on; the old ideas which were once so exciting to men's imaginations, now cease to move them, though they may be accepted as dull and necessary platitudes: the material circumstances of man's life which were once only struggled with in detail, and only according to a kind of law made manifest in their working, are in such times conscious of change, and are only accepted under protest until some means can be found to alter them. The old and dying order, once silent and all-powerful, tries to express itself violently, and becomes at once noisy and weak. The nascent order once too weak to be conscious of need of expression, or capable of it if it were, becomes conscious now and finds a voice. The silent sap of the years is being laid aside for open assault; the men are gathering under arms in the trenches, and the forlorn hope is ready, no longer trifling with little solacements of the time of weary waiting, but looking forward to mere death or the joy of victory.

Now I think, and some who read this will agree with me, that we are now living in one of these times of conscious change; we not only are, but we also feel ourselves to be living between the old and the new; we are expecting something to happen, as the phrase goes: at such times it behoves us to understand what is the old which is dying, what is the new which is coming into existence? That is a question practically important to us all, since these periods of conscious change are also, in one way or other, times of serious combat, and each of us, if he does not look to it and learn to understand what is going on, may find himself fighting on the wrong side, the side with which he really does not sympathize.

What is the combat we are now entering upon—who is it to be fought between? Absolutism and Democracy, perhaps some will answer. Not quite, I think; that contest was practically settled by the great French Revolution; it is only its embers which are burning now: or at least that is so in the countries which are not belated like Russia, for instance. Democracy, or at least what used to be considered Democracy, is now triumphant; and though it is true that there are countries where freedom of speech is repressed besides Russia, as e.g., Germany and Ireland, [176] that only happens when the rulers of the triumphant Democracy are beginning to be afraid of the new order of things, now becoming conscious of itself, and are being driven into reaction in consequence. No, it is not Absolutism and Democracy as the French Revolution understood those two words that are the enemies now: the issue is deeper than it was; the two foes are now Mastership and Fellowship. This is a far more serious quarrel than the old one, and involves a much completer revolution. The grounds of conflict are really quite different. Democracy said and says, men shall not be the masters of others, because hereditary privilege has made a race or a family so, and they happen to belong to such race; they shall individually grow into being the masters of others by the development of certain qualities under a system of authority which artificially protects the wealth of every man, if he has acquired it in accordance with this artificial system, from the interference of every other, or from all others combined.

The new order of things says, on the contrary, why have masters at all? let us be fellows working in the harmony of association for the common good, that is, for the greatest happiness and completest development of every human being in the community.

This ideal and hope of a new society founded on industrial peace and forethought, bearing with it its own ethics, aiming at a new and higher life for all men, has received the general name of Socialism, and it is my firm belief that it is destined to supersede the old order of things founded on industrial war, and to be the next step in the progress of humanity.

Now, since I must explain further what are the aims of Socialism, the ideal of the new epoch, I find that I must begin by explaining to you what is the constitution of the old order which it is destined to supplant. If I can make that clear to you, I shall have also made clear to you the first aim of Socialism: for I have said that the present and decaying order of things, like those which have gone before it, has to be propped up by a system of artificial authority; when that artificial authority has been swept away, harmonious association will be felt by all men to be a necessity of their happy and undegraded existence on the earth, and Socialism will become the condition under which we shall all live, and it will develop naturally, and probably with no violent conflict, whatever detailed system may be necessary: I say the struggle will not be over these details, which will surely vary according to the difference of unchangeable natural surroundings, but over the question, shall it be mastership or fellowship?

Let us see then what is the condition of society under the last development of mastership, the commercial system, which has taken the place of the Feudal system.

Like all other systems of society, it is founded on the necessity of man conquering his subsistence from Nature by labour, and also, like most other systems that we know of, it presupposes the unequal distribution of labour among different classes of society, and the unequal distribution of the results of that labour: it does not differ in that respect from the system which it supplanted; it has only altered the method whereby that unequal distribution should be arranged. There are still rich people and poor people amongst us, as there were in the Middle Ages; nay, there is no doubt that, relatively at least to the sum of wealth existing, the rich are richer and the poor are poorer now than they were then. However that may be, in any case now as then there are people who have much work and little wealth living beside other people who have much wealth and little work. The richest are still the idlest, and those who work hardest and perform the most painful tasks are the worst rewarded for their labour.

To me, and I should hope to my readers, this seems grossly unfair; and I may remind you here that the world has always had a sense of its injustice. For century after century, while society has strenuously bolstered up this injustice forcibly and artificially, it has professed belief in philosophies, codes of ethics, and religions which have inculcated justice and fair dealing between men: nay, some of them have gone so far as to bid us bear one another's burdens, and have put before men the duty, and in the long run the pleasure, of the strong working for the weak, the wise for the foolish, the helpful for the helpless; and yet these precepts of morality have been set aside in practice as persistently as they have been preached in theory; and naturally so, since they attack the very basis of class society. I as a Socialist am bound to preach them to you once more, assuring you that they are no mere foolish dreams bidding us to do what we now must acknowledge to be impossible, but reasonable rules of action, good for our defence against the tyranny of Nature. Anyhow, honest men have the choice before them of either putting these theories in practice or rejecting them altogether. If they will but face that dilemma, I think we shall soon have a new world of it; yet I fear they will find it hard to do so: the theory is old, and we have got used to it and its form of words: the practice is new, and would involve responsibilities we have not yet thought much of.

Now the great difference between our present system and that of the feudal period is that, as far as the conditions of life are concerned, all distinction of classes is abolished except that between rich and poor: society is thus simplified; the arbitrary distinction is gone, the real one remains and is far more stringent than the arbitrary one was. Once all society was rude, there was little real difference between the gentleman and the non-gentleman, and you had to dress them differently from one another in order to distinguish them. But now a well-to-do man is a refined and cultivated being, enjoying to the full his share of the conquest over Nature which the modern world has achieved, while the poor man is rude and degraded, and has no share in the wealth conquered by modern science from Nature: he is certainly no better as to material condition than the serf of the Middle Ages, perhaps he is worse: to my mind he is at least worse than the savage living in a good climate.

I do not think that any thoughtful man seriously denies this: let us try to see what brings it about; let us see it as clearly as we all see that the hereditary privilege of the noble caste, and the consequent serf slavery of the workers of the Middle Ages, brought about the peculiar conditions of that period.

Society is now divided between two classes, those who monopolize all the means of the production of wealth save one; and those who possess nothing except that one, the Power of Labour. That power of labour is useless to its possessors, and cannot be exercised without the help of the other means of production; but those who have nothing but labour-power—i.e., who have no means of making others work for them, must work for themselves in order to live; and they must therefore apply to the owners of the means of fructifying labour—i.e., the land, machinery, &c., for leave to work that they may live. The possessing class (as for short we will call them) are quite prepared to grant this leave, and indeed they must grant it if they are to use the labour-power of the non-possessing class for their own advantage, which is their special privilege. But that privilege enables them to compel the non-possessing class to sell them their labour-power on terms which ensure the continuance of their monopoly. These terms are at the outset very simple. The possessing class, or masters, allow the men just so much of the wealth produced by their labour as will give them such a livelihood as is considered necessary at the time, and will permit them to breed and rear children to a working age: that is the simple condition of the "bargain" which obtains when the labour-power required is low in quality, what is called unskilled labour, and when the workers are too weak or ignorant to combine so as to threaten the masters with some form of rebellion. When skilled labour is wanted, and the labourer has consequently cost more to produce, and is rarer to be found, the price of the article is higher: as also when the commodity labour takes to thinking and remembers that after all it is also men, and as aforesaid holds out threats to the masters; in that case they for their part generally think it prudent to give way, when the competition of the market allows them to do so, and so the standard of livelihood for the workers rises.

But to speak plainly, the greater part of the workers, in spite of strikes and Trades' Unions, do get little more than a bare subsistence wage, and when they grow sick or old they would die outright if it were not for the refuge afforded them by the workhouse, which is purposely made as prison-like and wretched as possible, in order to prevent the lower-paid workers from taking refuge in it before the time of their industrial death.

Now comes the question as to how the masters are able to force the men to sell their commodity labour-power so dirt-cheap without treating them as the ancients treated their slaves—i.e., with the whip. Well, of course you understand that the master having paid his workmen what they can live upon, and having paid for the wear and tear of machinery and other expenses of that kind, has for his share whatever remains over and above, the whole of which he gets from the exercise of the labour-power possessed by the worker: he is anxious therefore to make the most of this privilege, and competes with his fellow-manufacturers to the utmost in the market: so that the distribution of wares is organized on a gambling basis, and as a consequence many more hands are needed when trade is brisk than when it is slack, or even in an ordinary condition: under the stimulus also of the lust for acquiring this surplus value of labour, the great machines of our epoch were invented and are yearly improved, and they act on labour in a threefold way: first they get rid of many hands; next they lower the quality of the labour required, so that skilled work is wanted less and less; thirdly, the improvement in them forces the workers to work harder while they are at work, as notably in the cotton-spinning industry. Also in most trades women and children are employed, to whom it is not even pretended that a subsistence wage is given. Owing to all these causes, the reserve army of labour necessary to our present system of manufactures for the gambling market, the introduction of labour-saving machines (labour saved for the master, mind you, not the man), and the intensifying of the labour while it lasts, the employment of the auxiliary labour of women and children: owing to all this there are in ordinary years even, not merely in specially bad years like the current one, [184] more workers than there is work for them to do. The workers therefore undersell one another in disposing of their one commodity, labour-power, and are forced to do so, or they would not be allowed to work, and therefore would have to starve or go to the prison called the workhouse. This is why the masters at the present day are able to dispense with the exercise of obvious violence which in bygone times they used towards their slaves.

This then is the first distinction between the two great classes of modern Society: the upper class possesses wealth, the lower lacks wealth; but there is another distinction to which I will now draw your attention: the class which lacks wealth is the class that produces it, the class that possesses it does not produce it, it consumes it only. If by any chance the so-called lower class were to perish or leave the community, production of wealth would come to a standstill, until the wealth-owners had learned how to produce, until they had descended from their position, and had taken the place of their former slaves. If on the contrary, the wealth-owners were to disappear, production of wealth would at the worst be only hindered for awhile, and probably would go on pretty much as it does now.

But you may say, though it is certain that some of the wealth-owners, as landlords, holders of funds, and the like do nothing, yet there are many of them who work hard. Well, that is true, and perhaps nothing so clearly shows the extreme folly of the present system than this fact that there are so many able and industrious men employed by it, in working hard at—nothing: nothing or worse. They work, but they do not produce.

It is true that some useful occupations are in the hands of the privileged classes, physic, education, and the fine arts, e.g. The men who work at these occupations are certainly working usefully; and all that we can say against them is that they are sometimes paid too high in proportion to the pay of other useful persons, which high pay is given them in recognition of their being the parasites of the possessing classes. But even as to numbers these are not a very large part of the possessors of wealth, and, as to the wealth they hold, it is quite insignificant compared with that held by those who do nothing useful.

Of these last, some, as we all agree, do not pretend to do anything except amuse themselves, and probably these are the least harmful of the useless classes. Then there are others who follow occupations which would have no place in a reasonable condition of society, as, e.g., lawyers, judges, jailers, and soldiers of the higher grades, and most Government officials. Finally comes the much greater group of those who are engaged in gambling or fighting for their individual shares of the tribute which their class compels the working-class to yield to it: these are the group that one calls broadly business men, the conductors of our commerce, if you please to call them so.

To extract a good proportion of this tribute, and to keep as much as possible of it when extracted for oneself, is the main business of life for these men, that is, for most well-to-do and rich people; it is called, quite inaccurately, "money-making;" and those who are most successful in this occupation are, in spite of all hypocritical pretences to the contrary, the persons most respected by the public.

A word or two as to the tribute extracted from the workers as aforesaid. It is no trifle, but amounts to at least two-thirds of all that the worker produces; but you must understand that it is not all taken directly from the workman by his immediate employer, but by the employing class. Besides the tribute or profit of the direct employer, which is in all cases as much as he can get amidst his competition or war with other employers, the worker has also to pay taxes in various forms, and the greater part of the wealth so extorted is at the best merely wasted: and remember, whoever seems to pay the taxes, labour in the long run is the only real taxpayer. Then he has to pay house-rent, and very much heavier rent in proportion to his earnings than well-to-do people have. He has also to pay the commission of the middle-men who distribute the goods which he has made, in a way so wasteful that now all thinking people cry out against it, though they are quite helpless against it in our present society. Finally, he has often to pay an extra tax in the shape of a contribution to a benefit society or trades' union, which is really a tax on the precariousness of his employment caused by the gambling of his masters in the market. In short, besides the profit or the result of unpaid labour which he yields to his immediate master he has to give back a large part of his wages to the class of which his master is a part.

The privilege of the possessing class therefore consists in their living on this tribute, they themselves either not working or working unproductively—i.e., living on the labour of others; no otherwise than as the master of ancient days lived on the labour of his slave, or as the baron lived on the labour of his serf. If the capital of the rich man consists of land, he is able to force a tenant to improve his land for him and pay him tribute in the form of rack-rent; and at the end of the transaction has his land again, generally improved, so that he can begin again and go on for ever, he and his heirs, doing nothing, a mere burden on the community for ever, while others are working for him. If he has houses on his land he has rent for them also, often receiving the value of the building many times over, and in the end house and land once more. Not seldom a piece of barren ground or swamp, worth nothing in itself, becomes a source of huge fortune to him from the development of a town or a district, and he pockets the results of the labour of thousands upon thousands of men, and calls it his property: or the earth beneath the surface is found to be rich in coal or minerals, and again he must be paid vast sums for allowing others to labour them into marketable wares, to which labour he contributes nothing.

Or again, if his capital consists of cash, he goes into the labour market and buys the labour-power of men, women and children, and uses it for the production of wares which shall bring him in a profit, buying it of course at the lowest price that he can, availing himself of their necessities to keep their livelihood down to the lowest point which they will bear: which indeed he must do, or he himself will be overcome in the war with his fellow-capitalists. Neither in this case does he do any useful work, and he need not do any semblance of it, since he may buy the brain-power of managers at a somewhat higher rate than he buys the hand-power of the ordinary workman. But even when he does seem to be doing something, and receives the pompous title of "organizer of labour," he is not really organizing labour, but the battle with his immediate enemies, the other capitalists, who are in the same line of business with himself.

Furthermore, though it is true, as I have said, that the working-class are the only producers, yet only a part of them are allowed to produce usefully; for the men of the non-producing classes having often much more wealth than they can use are forced to waste it in mere luxuries and follies, that on the one hand harm themselves, and on the other withdraw a very large part of the workers from useful work, thereby compelling those who do produce usefully to work the harder and more grievously: in short, the essential accompaniment of the system is waste.

How could it be otherwise, since it is a system of war? I have mentioned incidentally that all the employers of labour are at war with each other, and you will probably see that, according to my account of the relations between the two great classes, they also are at war. Each can only gain at the others' loss: the employing class is forced to make the most of its privilege, the possession of the means for the exercise of labour, and whatever it gets to itself can only be got at the expense of the working-class; and that class in its turn can only raise its standard of livelihood at the expense of the possessing class; it is forced to yield as little tribute to it as it can help; there is therefore constant war always going on between these two classes, whether they are conscious of it or not.

To recapitulate: In our modern society there are two classes, a useful and a useless class; the useless class is called the upper, the useful the lower class. The useless or upper class, having the monopoly of all the means of the production of wealth save the power of labour, can and does compel the useful or lower class to work for its own disadvantage, and for the advantage of the upper class; nor will the latter allow the useful class to work on any other terms. This arrangement necessarily means an increasing contest, first of the classes one against the other, and next of the individuals of each class among themselves.

Most thinking people admit the truth of what I have just stated, but many of them believe that the system, though obviously unjust and wasteful, is necessary (though perhaps they cannot give their reasons for their belief), and so they can see nothing for it but palliating the worst evils of the system: but, since the various palliatives in fashion at one time or another have failed each in its turn, I call upon them, firstly, to consider whether the system itself might not be changed, and secondly, to look round and note the signs of approaching change.

Let us remember first that even savages live, though they have poor tools, no machinery, and no co-operation, in their work: but as soon as a man begins to use good tools and work with some kind of co-operation he becomes able to produce more than enough for his own bare necessaries, All industrial society is founded on that fact, even from the time when workmen were mere chattel slaves. What a strange society then is this of ours, wherein while one set of people cannot use their wealth, they have so much, but are obliged to waste it, another set are scarcely if at all better than those hapless savages who have neither tools nor co-operation! Surely if this cannot be set right, civilized mankind must write itself down a civilized fool.

Here is the workman now, thoroughly organized for production, working for production with complete co-operation, and through marvellous machines; surely if a slave in Aristotle's time could do more than keep himself alive, the present workman can do much more—as we all very well know that he can. Why therefore should he be otherwise than in a comfortable condition? Simply because of the class system, which with one hand plunders, and with the other wastes the wealth won by the workman's labour. If the workman had the full results of his labour he would in all cases be comfortably off, if he were working in an unwasteful way. But in order to work unwastefully he must work for his own livelihood, and not to enable another man to live without producing: if he has to sustain another man in idleness who is capable of working for himself, he is treated unfairly; and, believe me, he will only do so as long he is compelled to submit by ignorance and brute force. Well, then, he has a right to claim the wealth produced by his labour, and in consequence to insist that all shall produce who are able to do so; but also undoubtedly his labour must be organized, or he will soon find himself relapsing into the condition of the savage. But in order that his labour may be organized properly he must have only one enemy to contend with—Nature to wit, who as it were eggs him on to the conflict against herself, and is grateful to him for overcoming her; a friend in the guise of an enemy. There must be no contention of man with man, but association instead; so only can labour be really organized, harmoniously organized. But harmony cannot co-exist with contention for individual gain: men must work for the common gain if the world is to be raised out of its present misery; therefore that claim of the workman (that is of every able man) must be subject to the fact that he is but a part of a harmonious whole: he is worthless without the co-operation of his fellows, who help him according to their capacities: he ought to feel, and will feel when he has his right senses, that he is working for his own interest when he is working for that of the community.

So working, his work must always be profitable, therefore no obstacle must be thrown in the way of his work: the means whereby his labour-power can be exercised must be free to him. The privilege of the proprietary class must come to an end. Remember that at present the custom is that a person so privileged is in the position of a man (with a policeman or so to help) guarding the gate of a field which will supply livelihood to whomsoever can work in it: crowds of people who don't want to die come to that gate; but there stands law and order, and says "pay me five shillings before you go in;" and he or she that hasn't the five shillings has to stay outside, and die—or live in the workhouse. Well, that must be done away with; the field must be free to everybody that can use it. To throw aside even this transparent metaphor, those means of the fructification of labour, the land, machinery, capital, means of transit, &c., which are now monopolized by those who cannot use them, but who abuse them to force unpaid labour out of others, must be free to those who can use them; that is to say, the workers properly organized for production; but you must remember that this will wrong no man, because as all will do some service to the community—i.e., as there will be no non-producing class, the organized workers will be the whole community, there will be no one left out.

Society will thus be recast, and labour will be free from all compulsion except the compulsion of Nature, which gives us nothing for nothing. It would be futile to attempt to give you details of the way in which this would be carried out; since the very essence of it is freedom and the abolition of all arbitrary or artificial authority; but I will ask you to understand one thing: you will no doubt want to know what is to become of private property under such a system, which at first sight would not seem to forbid the accumulation of wealth, and along with that accumulation the formation of new classes of rich and poor.

Now private property as at present understood implies the holding of wealth by an individual as against all others, whether the holder can use it or not: he may, and not seldom he does, accumulate capital, or the stored-up labour of past generations, and neither use it himself nor allow others to use it: he may, and often he does, engross the first necessity of labour, land,

and neither use it himself or allow any one else to use it; and though it is clear that in each case he is injuring the community, the law is sternly on his side. In any case a rich man accumulates property, not for his own use, but in order that he may evade with impunity the law of Nature which bids man labour for his livelihood, and also that he may enable his children to do the same, that he and they may belong to the upper or useless class: it is not wealth that he accumulates, well-being, well-doing, bodily and mental; he soon comes to the end of his real needs in that respect, even when they are most exacting: it is power over others, what our forefathers called riches, that he collects; power (as we have seen) to force other people to live for his advantage poorer lives than they should live. Understand that that must be the result of the possession of riches.

Now this power to compel others to live poorly Socialism would abolish entirely, and in that sense would make an end of private property: nor would it need to make laws to prevent accumulation artificially when once people had found out that they could employ themselves, and that thereby every man could enjoy the results of his own labour: for Socialism bases the rights of the individual to possess wealth on his being able to use that wealth for his own personal needs, and, labour being properly organized, every person, male or female, not in nonage or otherwise incapacitated from working, would have full opportunity to produce wealth and thereby to satisfy his own personal needs; if those needs went in any direction beyond those of an average man, he would have to make personal sacrifices in order to satisfy them; he would have, for instance, to work longer hours, or to forego some luxury that he did not care for in order to obtain something which he very much desired: so doing he would at the worst injure no one: and you will clearly see that there is no other choice for him between so doing and his forcing some one else to forego his special desires; and this latter proceeding by the way, when it is done without the sanction of the most powerful part of society, is called theft; though on the big scale and duly sanctioned by artificial laws, it is, as we have seen, the groundwork of our present system. Once more, that system refuses permission to people to produce unless under artificial restrictions; under Socialism, every one who could produce would be free to produce, so that the price of an article would be just the cost of its production, and what we now call profit would no longer exist: thus, for instance, if a person wanted chairs, he would accumulate them till he had as many as he could use, and then he would stop, since he would not have been able to buy them for less than their cost of production and could not sell them for more: in other words, they would be nothing else than chairs; under the present system they may be means of compulsion and destruction as formidable as loaded rifles.

No one therefore would dispute with a man the possession of what he had acquired without injury to others, and what he could use without injuring them, and it would so remove temptations toward the abuse of possession, that probably no laws would be necessary to prevent it.

A few words now as to the differentiation of reward of labour, as I know my readers are sure to want an exposition of the Socialist views here as to those who direct labour or who have specially excellent faculties towards production. And, first, I will look on the super-excellent workman as an article presumably needed by the community; and then say that, as with other articles so with this, the community must pay the cost of his production: for instance, it will have to seek him out, to develop his special capacities, and satisfy any needs he may have (if any) beyond those of an average man, so long as the satisfaction of those needs is not hurtful to the community.

Furthermore, you cannot give him more than he can use so he will not ask for more, and will not take it: it is true that his work may be more special than another's, but it is not more necessary if you have organized labour properly; the ploughman and the fisherman are as necessary to society as the scientist or the artist, I will not say more necessary: neither is the difficulty of producing the more special and excellent work at all proportionate to its speciality or excellence: the higher workman produces his work as easily perhaps as the lower does his work; if he does not do so, you must give him extra leisure, extra means for supplying the waste of power in him, but you can give him nothing more. The only reward that you can give the excellent workman is opportunity for developing and exercising his excellent capacity. I repeat, you can give him nothing more worth his having: all other rewards are either illusory or harmful. I must say in passing, that our present system of dealing with what is called a man of genius is utterly absurd: we cruelly starve him and repress his capacity when he is young; we foolishly pamper and flatter him and again repress his capacity when he is middle-aged or old: we get the least out of him, not the most.

These last words concern mere rarities in the way of workmen; but in this respect it is only a matter of degree; the point of the whole thing is this, that the director of labour is in his place because he is fit for it, not by a mere accident; being fit for it, he does it easier than he would do other work, and needs no more compensation for the wear and tear of life than another man does, and not needing it will not claim it, since it would be no use to him; his special reward for his special labour is, I repeat, that he can do it easily, and so does not feel it a burden; nay, since he can do it well he likes doing it, since indeed the main pleasure of life is the exercise of energy in the development of our special capacities. Again, as regards the workmen who are under his direction, he needs no special dignity or authority; they know well enough that so long as he fulfils his function and really does direct them, if they do not heed him it will be at the cost of their labour being more irksome and harder. All this, in short, is what is meant by the organization of labour, which is, in other words, finding out what work such and such people are fittest for and leaving them free to do that: we won't take the trouble to do that now, with the result that people's best faculties are wasted, and that work is a heavy burden to them, which they naturally shirk as much as they can; it should be rather a pleasure to them: and I say straight out that, unless we find some means to make all work more or less pleasurable, we shall never escape from the great tyranny of the modern world.

Having mentioned the difference between the competitive and commercial ideas on the subject of the individual holding of wealth and the relative position of different groups of workmen, I will very briefly say something on what for want of a better word I must call the political position which we take up, or at least what we look forward to in the long run. The substitution of association for competition is the foundation of Socialism, and will run through all acts done under it, and this must act as between nations as well as between individuals: when profits can no more be made, there will be no necessity for holding together masses of men to draw together the greatest proportion of profit to their locality, or to the real or imaginary union of persons and corporations which is now called a nation. What we now call a nation is a body whose function it is to assert the special welfare of its incorporated members at the expense of all other similar bodies: the death of competition will deprive it of this function; since there will be no attack there need be no defence, and it seems to me that this function being taken away from the nation it can have no other, and therefore must cease to exist as a political entity. On this side of the movement opinion is growing steadily. It is clear that, quite apart from Socialism, the idea of local administration is pushing out that of centralized government: to take a remarkable case: in the French Revolution of 1793, the most advanced party was centralizing: in the latest French revolution, that of the Commune of 1871, it was federalist. Or take Ireland, the success which is to-day attending the struggles of Ireland for independence is, I am quite sure, owing to the spread of this idea: it no longer seems a monstrous proposition to liberal-minded Englishmen that a country should administer its own affairs: the feeling that it is not only just, but also very convenient to all parties for it to do so, is extinguishing the prejudices fostered by centuries of oppressive and wasteful mastership. And I believe that Ireland will show that her claim for self-government is not made on behalf of national rivalry, but rather on behalf of genuine independence; the consideration, on the one hand, of the needs of her own population, and, on the other, goodwill towards that of other localities. Well, the spread of this idea will make our political work as Socialists the easier; men will at last come to see that the only way to avoid the tyranny and waste of bureaucracy is by the Federation of Independent Communities: their federation being for definite purposes: for furthering the organization of labour, by ascertaining the real demand for commodities, and so avoiding waste: for organizing the distribution of goods, the migration of persons—in short, the friendly intercommunication of people whose interests are common, although the circumstances of their natural surroundings made necessary differences of life and manners between them.

I have thus sketched something of the outline of Socialism, by showing that its aim is first to get rid of the monopoly of the means of fructifying labour, so that labour may be free to all, and its resulting wealth may not be engrossed by a few, and so cause the misery and degradation of the many: and, secondly, that it aims at organizing labour so that none of it may be wasted, using as a means thereto the free development of each man's capacity; and, thirdly, that it aims at getting rid of national rivalry, which in point of fact means a condition of perpetual war, sometimes of the money-bag, sometimes of the bullet, and substituting for this worn-out superstition a system of free communities living in harmonious federation with each other, managing their own affairs by the free consent of their members; yet acknowledging some kind of centre whose function it would be to protect the principle whose practice the communities should carry out; till at last those principles would be recognized by every one always and intuitively, when the last vestiges of centralization would die out.

I am well aware that this complete Socialism, which is sometimes called Communism, cannot be realized all at once; society will be changed from its basis when we make the form of robbery called profit impossible by giving labour full and free access to the means of its fructification—i.e., to raw material. The demand for this emancipation of labour is the basis on which all Socialists may unite. On more indefinite grounds they cannot meet other groups of politicians; they can only rejoice at seeing the ground cleared of controversies which are really dead, in order that the last controversy may be settled that we can at present foresee, and the question solved as to whether or no it is necessary, as some people think it is, that society should be composed of two groups of dishonest persons, slaves submitting to be slaves, yet for ever trying to cheat their masters, and masters conscious of their having no support for their dishonesty of eating the common stock without adding to it save the mere organization of brute force, which they have to assert for ever in all details of life against the natural desire of man to be free.

It may be hoped that we of this generation may be able to prove that it is unnecessary; but it will, doubt it not, take many generations yet to prove that it is necessary for such degradation to last as long as humanity does; and when that is finally proved we shall at least have one hope left—that humanity will not last long.

FOOTNOTES.

[13] Falsely; because the privileged classes have at their back the force of the Executive by means of which to compel the unprivileged to accept their terms; if this is "free competition" there is no meaning in words.

[37a] Read at the Conference convened by the Fabian Society at South Place Institute, June 11, 1886.

[37b] They have been "rather rough," you may say, and have done more than merely hold their sentimental position. Well, I still say (February 1888) that the present open tyranny which sends political opponents to prison, both in England and Ireland, and breaks Radical heads in the street for attempting to attend political meetings, is not Tory, but Whig; not the old Tory "divine right of kings," but the new Tory, i.e., Tory-tinted Whig, "divine right of property" made Bloody Sunday possible. I admit that I did not expect in 1886 that we should in 1887 and 1888 be having such a brilliant example of the tyranny of a parliamentary majority; in fact, I did not reckon on the force of the impenetrable stupidity of the Prigs in alliance with the Whigs marching under the rather ragged banner of sham Toryism.

[43] As true now (February 1888) as then: the murder of the Chicago Anarchists, to wit.

[87] I suppose he was speaking of the frame houses of Kent.

[176] And the brick and mortar country London, also, it seems (Feb. 1888).

[184] 1886, to wit.

Note from the Editor

Odin's Library Classics strives to bring you unedited and unabridged works of classical literature. As such, this is the complete and unabridged version of the original English text unless noted. In some instances, obvious typographical errors have been corrected. This is done to preserve the original text as much as possible. The English language has evolved since the writing and some of the words appear in their original form, or at least the most commonly used form at the time. This is done to protect the original intent of the author. If at any time you are unsure of the meaning of a word, please do your research on the etymology of that word. It is important to preserve the history of the English language.

Taylor Anderson

30123889R00046

Printed in Great Britain
by Amazon